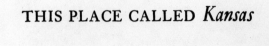

THIS PLACE CALLED *Kansas*

THIS PLACE

 NORMAN

CALLED

KANSAS

by Charles C. Howes

UNIVERSITY OF OKLAHOMA PRESS

[*This Place Called Kansas* was first published in a substantial edition in the fall of 1952 and was reprinted within eight months. Throughout the ensuing years it enjoyed a steady sale. As the Kansas centennial year 1961 approached, however, the demand not only continued but increased. It seemed appropriate, therefore, to make a new printing available as part of the publisher's contribution to the Kansas celebration of a century of statehood.

Charles C. Howes, the assistant director of the Kansas Centennial Commission, produced his delightful account of the social and cultural pattern of Kansas largely from writings and notes by his late father, Cecil Howes. It is gratifying to be able to reissue the book on a sister state which both father and son lovingly describe in this eye-witness record.—*University of Oklahoma Press.*]

The Why and Wherefore

No work of authorship, so far as I know, has been simpler or easier of accomplishment than this book. It was developed from the notes, writings, and papers left by my father, Cecil Howes, after almost half a century of active newspaper reporting, nearly all of it in Kansas. He had already done what it would have taken me an equal lifetime to do, had I been also so fortunate as to have lived in his time rather than mine: he had absorbed much of the historical background, sentiments, and habits that started Kansas on the road to greatness.

As he traveled Kansas and talked with the old-timers, whom the late Bent Murdock called "The Sovereign Squats," some of whom had come to the state during Squatter Sovereignty days, he heard much of the lore, traditions, and tales of the men and women of the state. Some of this is, of course, apocryphal. But in the main the facts and their sources were carefully noted and verified by "Cece" Howes. It has been my purpose, in putting the book together, to recheck everything rather carefully and to bring information up to date when necessary.

The Kansas lore that Cecil Howes gathered was the product very largely of more than forty years of his reporting for the

Kansas City Star. For this entire period, he was statehouse correspondent in Topeka. Thus, when Kansans did something, it was necessary for the *Star* to find out why, and Howes was sent scurrying for the history.

Since Kansans have always been doing something, the experience gained in background writing brought my father into view as popular historian and chronicler. In his later years he began a series of monthly articles on Kansas for *The Kansas Teacher.* A large part of this book is taken from his work for that magazine and the *Star,* collected and edited with much more than a passive interest on my part.

The Kansas historical library and newspaper section was a regular port of call on the Howes beat, and the staff members and officers of the Kansas State Historical Society were diligent in helping him to unearth the musty writings of yesterday. The reporter himself had assembled a historical collection of some five hundred volumes for his own private collection.

There are many chronologies of Kansas history, but there are few eye-witness records of the kind Father kept, bringing color and an individuality that can only be described as "Kansan." Throughout the sixty years he was a resident of the state, "Cece" Howes never apologized for Kansas and often said that if Kansans knew more about the elements that made their state great they would stop feeling sorry for themselves. He had his eye on the means for bringing that change about when he started assembling the materials for this book, the final preparation of which I took over at his death.

CHARLES C. HOWES

Topeka, Kansas
March 15, 1952

Contents

Illustrations

Maps

THIS PLACE CALLED KANSAS:

I. *How It Started*

1: *In the Long, Long Ago*

THE EARLIEST recorded history of the area that is now Kansas comes to us from the visit of Coronado in 1541. It is a familiar story. He was commissioned by the governor of Mexico to go north in search of the Seven Cities of Cibola, especially Quivira, the richest city of all, where the streets were said to be paved with gold and the houses had precious stones imbedded in their doors.

Coronado spent a winter in New Mexico and then started eastward from his winter quarters near present Albuquerque. Some of his men had been cruel to the natives, who most heartily wanted to get rid of the conquistadores. An Indian guide was found who told the Spaniards that he knew the way to Quivira and would lead the mighty army to the land of gold and milk and honey.

The Indian led Coronado and his army to the Staked Plains of Texas, the high and dry area of the western part of that great state. After wandering for a month, some of Coronado's men discovered that they had crossed tracks they had made many days earlier and disclosed to Coronado that the army had been led in a circle over the plains country in the expectation that the entire army would perish from hunger and thirst.

The Indian guide was murdered at once, and an Indian of another tribe, who said he was headed for home, agreed to act as guide. Coronado sent part of his army back to the winter quarters to await his return and, with a small group of thirty men, started north.

That Coronado reached Kansas is a well-established fact. His journal and that of the historian of the expedition, Jaramillo, tell of the march northward over the prairies, through great herds of humpbacked cattle, the first any of the Spaniards had seen. On the feast day of St. Peter and St. Paul, June 29, 1541, the journals of the expedition show that the group came to the largest river they had crossed in all their wanderings over the plains. The party crossed the river, and after naming it the River of St. Peter and St. Paul in observance of the day, started down the north bank.

This crossing of the Arkansas River is believed to have been near what is now the town of Spearville. The journals go on to note that the party followed along the north bank of the river, which flowed to the southeast. Two or three leagues beyond the point of the crossing the river made an abrupt turn to the northeast. The party followed the river northeastward for about thirty leagues until the river swung to the southeast again. An examination of any map of the Great Plains area discloses that the Arkansas River is the only stream coming out of the mountains which, after flowing southeast some two hundred miles, makes an abrupt turn to the northeast. It is this geographical fact that has brought complete accord among historians that Coronado and his party moved as far into present Kansas as the top of the great bend in the Arkansas River.

The journey to the north and east from the point where the river turns southeast is not definitely fixed, since the journals of the expedition are rather incomplete and indefinite. Some historians assert that Coronado never went beyond a point near present Lyons, in Rice County. Others assert that he crossed the Smoky Hill River and went as far north as the

4

fortieth parallel and conclude that the Quivira he visited was the Pawnee Indian village on the Republican River near Belleville. Still others are just as certain that Quivira was located along the Smoky Hill River somewhere between Salina and Junction City. There is an Indian burial ground east of Salina which adds some credence to the belief that the village was near by. There are some who assert that exploring parties sent out by Coronado went as far east as the Missouri River somewhere along the northeastern border of Kansas. The Quivira Historical Society of Junction City has erected a monument which is claimed to mark the farthest point east and north to which Coronado traveled. A great hill southwest of Salina is named Coronado Heights, and it is asserted that the conquistador climbed this hill and discovered the great valley beyond and the Indian village of Quivira.

The second guide for the expedition told Coronado there wasn't any gold or silver among the Indians of the prairie country, but the Spaniards wanted to see for themselves. Coronado spent a month or more in Kansas and doubtless sent out small groups to explore the country. His journal extols the virtues of the Indian lands at considerable length. He said that the land was the blackest loam he had ever seen and that it would grow all the grains, vegetables, and fruits common to Spain and would produce in greater abundance than any of the lands of Spain.

For nearly two hundred years after the visit of Coronado the Great Plains were visited by a small number of French and Spanish explorers, hunters, and trappers. They wandered across what is now Kansas and other states, mapping the area and claiming it for their respective kings. When Virginia was established as a colony of the British crown the grant included all the lands between the thirty-eighth and fortieth parallels "from ocean to ocean." This is about the only claim that the English ever made to the lands embracing present Kansas. The English made no explorations of the area, and no hunters or trappers from Virginia came far into the Middle West or attempted in any way to exercise the claims to the country for their king.

The French ranged up and down the Mississippi River and often came into Kansas. Bourgmont made the most extensive survey of the area and spent many months along the Arkansas, the Missouri, the Kaw, and as far north as the Platte River in Nebraska. The Spaniards sent out numerous expeditions from Mexico and established villages in Texas and New Mexico. Exploring parties came up into Kansas and probably into Nebraska. But they established no permanent settlements.

Most of the area of present Kansas was a part of the Louisiana Territory, which changed hands many times between Spain and France during the Napoleonic Wars. When the American colonies had made good their independence from England and Napoleon needed money to continue his conquests, he sold Louisiana to the United States for fifteen million dollars. This brought to the United States all of the Mississippi Valley, the Great Plains, and the area extending to the northwest across the Rocky Mountains to the Pacific and south of the Canadian border.

Most of Kansas was included in this purchase, except for the section of Kansas west of the hundredth meridian (Dodge City) and south of the Arkansas River, which was a part of the Spanish possessions. When Texas gained its independence from Mexico it was believed that this area properly belonged to the new republic. However, Texas did not claim it.

Thus the southwestern corner of Kansas, comprising nearly a dozen counties, all that part of the state west of the hundredth meridian and south of the Arkansas River, can rightfully claim to have been under five flags previous to that of the United States. Great Britain, Spain, France, Texas, and Mexico all had some claim to jurisdiction over this area. None except that of Mexico should be regarded as having much validity.

After the completion of the Louisiana Purchase the United States decided to explore the new possession. The Lewis and

Clark Expedition up the Missouri River was the first United States expedition to reach Kansas. This party celebrated July 4, 1804, at Isle du Vac (Cow Island) near the present site of Atchison and named the creek there "Independence Creek." The members of the expedition were in contact with the Kaw Indians, and the journals of the expedition show wide variation in the spelling of the name of this tribe, from which Kansas gets its name. It may be noted here that there are fifty-four different spellings for "Kansas" other than that accepted at the present time. The first spelling of "Kansas" in that form is found in the journals of the Lewis and Clark Expedition. It was also spelled Konza, Konga, Kanza, Kau, and Kaw. After a visit to the territory Rev. Isaac McCoy, an early-day Baptist missionary, found that the best rendering of the pronunciation of the name of the Indian tribe in the area was "Kauzau."

Lieutenant Zebulon Pike was sent out in 1806 with an army detachment to explore the prairie country. He visited the Pawnee Indians at a village on the Republican River near present Belleville and persuaded the Indians to take down the Spanish flag they were using and fly the American flag, after convincing them that they were now under the jurisdiction of the United States and owed no allegiance to Spain.

Major Stephen H. Long was another army explorer who traveled across Kansas in 1819–20. His route through the region was somewhat south of Pike's and took him and his party into what is now the panhandle of Texas and Oklahoma.

Both army men were disappointed in the high-plains area and submitted reports to the government that the lands comprising the area of Kansas west of the ninety-eighth meridian were practically worthless. They admitted that the high prairies afforded excellent pasturage for millions of bison, but they did not believe they were of any value for human habitation. In fact, Pike suggested that the plains' chief asset would be to provide a barrier against settlement of the mountain regions, which did not appear to him to be of any value whatever.

The Santa Fé Trail was the earliest and the most glamorous of the important highways which were established across Kansas. The eastern terminal was originally New Franklin, Missouri, then successively Arrow Rock, Independence, and finally Westport. Captain William Becknell was the first known traveler over the trail that was subsequently to prove so important. In 1821 he took a considerable amount of calico, clothes, trinkets, and equipment which he thought the Indians would buy and went to Santa Fé, New Mexico, that land of enchantment where the Spanish and Mexicans had mingled with the Pueblo Indians and established an unusually brilliant civilization of their own.

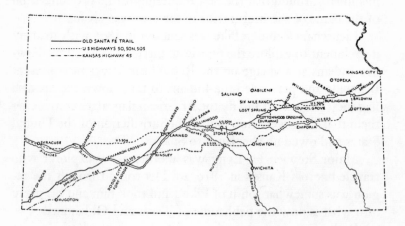

Becknell's reports of successful trading at Santa Fé sent other adventurers over the trail, and by 1825 business had become so large and profitable that the government sent out a commission to make a treaty with the Osage Indians for the unmolested use of the trail through the Osage lands. Later the trail route was surveyed by government engineers, and several forts were established to provide protection to the trail caravans from marauding Indians and others who might undertake raids on the rich treasure carried to and from Santa Fé.

Business on the trail grew into one of the most extensive freight movements in the country, employing thousands of men, horses, and mules. At one time several thousand oxen were used. Actually, there were three epochs in the development of the trail. The first was symbolized by the pack mule, the second by the ox team, and the third and last by the horse and mule. In the last period stagecoach facilities were also provided for passengers who desired to see Santa Fé and the mountain country and to explore the possibilities of establishing trading facilities in the Southwest.

The Santa Fé Trail flourished up to the period of the Civil War, was resumed at the close of that period, and continued to some extent until the Santa Fé railroad was built in the seventies. Its track followed generally the route of the old trail across Kansas, the southeastern corner of Colorado, and into New Mexico and provided such speedy and comfortable transportation that the stagecoach and the picturesque Conestoga wagon disappeared from the Kansas scene.

The Oregon and the California trails also started at Westport, Missouri, and followed the Santa Fé route for some miles into Kansas. There the Santa Fé trail turned to the southwest, while the Oregon and California trails turned to the northwest, crossing the Kansas or Kaw River near where Topeka now stands, either on the Pappan ferry when the river was high, or by fording it across rock ledges at two points, one above and one below Topeka.

The Oregon Trail followed the Kaw River bottoms to the Vermillion, thence northwest to cross the Blue River near Marysville, and thence into Nebraska, meeting the Mormon and California trails, which followed the Platte west from Omaha.

The Colorado Trail started at St. Joseph, Missouri, and went west along the present northern border of Kansas. It did not become an important trail until gold and silver were discovered in the Colorado Mountains, when the gold rush brought traffic in vast volume over that route. The Pony Express operated over the Colorado Trail from St. Joseph to the point where the Oregon-California Trail turned north after crossing the Blue River. The state of Kansas now owns the Pony Express station near Hanover, the last one before the route turned toward the Platte. The state has restored the old tavern and has made the area a state park.

A few settlers moved into the Indian Territory with the missionaries. Most of them were government agents or instructors who came to teach the Indians how to farm, do their own blacksmithing, and build their own homes. Many staked claims and remained as settlers in Kansas when the Kansas-Nebraska bill was enacted by Congress and the two new territories were opened to settlement. The government at once began to extinguish the Indian titles to the tribal lands, making allotments to those Indians who desired to stay and become citizens and moving the remnants of the other tribes to the Indian Territory or elsewhere. Many Indians and half-bloods who had established their own trading posts or operated ferries or conducted farm operations decided to remain in the new territories.

2: *The Original Owners*

A T THE time Coronado began the long trek to Quivira (which he found did not have streets paved with gold, doorknobs bespangled with jewels, and utensils made of solid silver), it appears probable that there were only three Indian tribes living permanently in Kansas—the Pawnees, the Kaws, and the Osages—although other tribes entered the area on hunting trips.

When Pike visited Kansas after the Louisiana Purchase, he found the Pawnees living in a permanent village on the Republican River near the north line of the state. The Kaw Indians long had lived in the valley of the river which bears their name and had roamed over a vast territory. They were generally recognized by other Indians as holding some title to the lands west of the Missouri River, north of the Kaw, south of the Platte, and east of the Big Blue. Other tribes came into the Kaw Valley for many years to obtain their winter supply of wild potatoes, which grew in the valley. The Kaw or Kansas River long bore the name "Topeka," which is, according to some authorities, an Indian word meaning "a good place to dig potatoes." When the eastern boundary of the Kaw Reservation was fixed and the army sent out surveyors to establish the lines, the maps used by Major Angus L. Langham showed the eastern reservation line to be twenty leagues up the Topeka River from its confluence with the Missouri. This reservation was later given to the Potawatomi Indians when the Kaws were moved from their original holdings to a new reservation around Council Grove.

For the most part, the Osages lived in present Missouri, along the Osage River in that state, but they occupied also some villages along the Marais des Cygnes, the Neosho, and possibly other streams in eastern Kansas.

There were no fixed boundaries for the lands belonging to any Indian tribe, and the Indians moved about freely to hunt or fish. There were frequent visits by members of other tribes, many of them coming from considerable distances. These wandering groups were generally on hunting or fishing expeditions or in search of better wild plant food. The only permanent Indian settlement in the western half of the state was at El Quartelejo in Scott County, where there was a small group of Pueblo Indians who had some time before moved away from the tribes of the far Southwest to establish a home of their own in this area.

Just when the Wichita tribe set up their village of grass huts at the confluence of the Big and Little Arkansas rivers has not been definitely determined. Many explorers and traders who came into the area found this small village or heard about it. The Wichitas were of a different stock from either the Osages or the Kaws, who belonged to the Siouan group. The Wichitas were Plains Indians, remnants of tribes that had inhabited areas as far south as the Brazos River in Texas. Some of the original tribe were said to have a marked resemblance in language and customs to tribes in Oregon. Among the Wichitas of Kansas, besides the original race, were Wacos and Tawakonies, who spoke the Wichita language, Kichais, who spoke a related language, and the Caddos, Ionies, and Nadakos (Anadarkos), who spoke the Caddo language. The outbreak of the Civil War caused them to move northward, gathering in southeast Kansas, and moving westward as the buffalo moved.

President Thomas Jefferson may be said to have conceived the idea of moving the Indian tribes of the eastern states to the far West, and it has been surmised that one compelling reason for his urgency in the purchase of the Louisiana Territory was to provide a suitable home for vast numbers of aborigines. There was dangerous unrest among these tribes, who were chafing bitterly at the encroachments of the white man and who threatened to halt the advance of settlement.

As the tide of immigration rolled westward beyond the Blue Ridge into the Ohio Valley and the Great Lakes region, the government took steps to extinguish the titles which the Indians claimed to these lands. It had to fight a severe war with some Indian tribes before this could be accomplished, and in the meantime the states of Missouri and Arkansas were being created.

So it was determined that the Indians of the eastern states

would be moved beyond the Mississippi. Finally, all the vast territory west and south of the Missouri River and west of the western borders of Missouri and Arkansas was designated as the Indian Territory. It was proposed to move all the tribes out of the east and the Northwest Territory to the new Indian Territory, which was to become the perpetual home of the Indians. But it remained their home for only about thirty years, when Kansas and Nebraska were formed into territories and the area south of the Kansas line and north of the Red River became the Indian Territory.

Among the more broad-minded government officials and statesmen of the formative years of the nation, doubtless there were some who expected, perhaps believed, that an Indian state would be created in the West which would become an integral part of the United States, governed by Indians for Indians. The project never materialized. The Indians, moved from their native habitat into a new land and often among new neighbors, were forced to become acclimated to unfamiliar conditions to satisfy the insatiable and unscrupulous desires of the white men and the political needs of the proponents on both sides of the great slavery question then materializing in Congress.

President Jackson told the eastern Indians to be prepared to move to the West. His emissaries said they could go peaceably or by compulsion, whichever they desired. Most of the tribes agreed to go without protest, but a few resisted, some of them successfully, the efforts to uproot them.

The story of the treatment of the Indians is not a pretty one and does no credit to the United States in most particulars. The white man was avaricious and found the red man, who was unable to bargain with him, a ready victim of the nefarious schemes of those who wanted the lands for themselves. The excuse that the Indian was unprogressive, uncivilized, and unable to adapt himself to the "American way of life" was not valid. Many Indians demonstrated that assimilation was possible, provided proper attention was paid to their education.

The approach was generally ineffective. The Indian had led a nomadic life for centuries, and here was a civilization superimposed upon him that sharply changed his mode of life and demanded of him many things which he did not understand.

Besides all this, the white man was fearful of the Indian. There had been some atrocities, and many of the white men proceeded to act on the well-worn doctrine that only dead Indians were good Indians by aiding in every possible way the dispersal of the tribes whose lands they coveted.

The first treaties involving the Kaws and the Osages were written in 1825 when the Kaws were moved back from the Missouri River to a reservation that began where Gage Boulevard in Topeka now stands and extended westward indefinitely. The Osages were moved out of Missouri and were to have lands along the Neosho—actually the greater part of southeastern Kansas.

The fear in which the Indians were held was well illustrated by two actions: the Platte Purchase and the creation of a neutral zone thirty miles wide along the western border of Missouri and Arkansas in which neither the Indian nor the white man could settle. The Platte Purchase involved the buying of the lands of the Iowas and the Sac and Fox tribes in northwestern Missouri and the moving of the western boundary of that state over to the Missouri River, which was expected to form a natural barrier against the Indian tribes who might raid the fast-settling area. Another treaty was written with the Osages whereby a right of way for the Santa Fé Trail was granted for the vast trade which had developed between the United States and Mexico. When the two treaties with the Kaws and the Osages were written and approved, the movement of the eastern tribes to the new territory got under way. The Indians insisted that the treaties guarantee that they would hold their new lands as long as "the grass should grow and the water should run."

There were many who believed that isolation was better

for the Indians. The policy of placing them on reservations seemed to be the only method whereby they could be spared complete moral degradation and ultimate extinction.

Rev. Isaac McCoy, for many years a missionary from the Baptist Church to the Indians in the Northwest Territory, led a committee of Indians from that area to Kansas to look over the lands proposed to be set aside for them. There were at least two important objections which McCoy offered to the removal. One was that the climatic change from damp, wooded areas to the hot plains would be unhealthful for the Indians. The other objection he had was the absence of hard maple trees to furnish them with sweetening for their food.

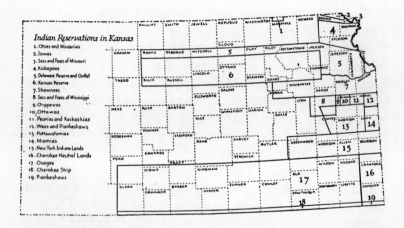

Indian Reservations in Kansas
1. Otoes and Missourias
2. Iowas
3. Sacs and Foxes of Missouri
4. Kickapoos
5. Delaware Reserve and Outlet
6. Kansas Reserve
7. Shawnees
8. Sacs and Foxes of Mississippi
9. Chippewas
10. Ottawas
11. Peorias and Kaskaskias
12. Weas and Piankeshaws
13. Pottawatomies
14. Miamias
15. New York Indians Lands
16. Cherokee Neutral Lands
17. Osages
18. Cherokee Strip
19. Piankeshaws

The first of the Indian tribes to be moved to the lands of the Kaws and the Osages were the Shawnees. They were followed by the Delawares, Ottawas, Peorias, Kaskaskias, Weas, Piankashaws, Quapaws, Cherokees, Chippewas, Kickapoos, Iowas, Sac and Foxes of Missouri, Potawatomis, Miamis, Sac and Foxes of Mississippi, Wyandottes, and the Munsees.

The Treaty of Buffalo Creek in 1838 provided for the removal of the Senecas, Onondagas, Cayugas, Tuscaroras, Oneidas, St. Regis, Stockbridges, Munsees, and Brothertons from New York to Wisconsin and then to Kansas, where a large area of land north of the Osages was set aside for them. But the New York Indians never came, and the lands were later declared public domain and opened for settlement.

With the formation of Kansas Territory in 1854 the government again began to extinguish Indian titles to the Kansas lands and move the tribes to the Indian Territory, the lands south of Kansas Territory and north of Texas. The settlement of some scores of tribes in this territory practically drained Kansas of its aboriginal population. Grant Foreman has given in graphic detail the process of removal for these people, gathered from as far away as Florida in the southeast to New York in the northeast, in two books, *Indian Removal* (1932) and *The Last Trek of the Indians* (1943).

In 1952 there were only about two thousand Indians residing in Kansas. The greater portion of these were the Potawatomis, who were quartered on their reservation in Jackson County, and the Kickapoos, Sac and Foxes and Iowas in Brown and Doniphan counties. Except for the Potawatomis, most of the Indians in Kansas live on their own farms or conduct their own business enterprises and have assumed full responsibilities as citizens of Kansas. They have their own homes, generally attend the schools of the community, and are active in community affairs to the same extent as other residents. The government maintains an extensive educational plant at the Haskell Indian Institute, Lawrence, which is attended by Indians from tribes throughout the Southwest. Some Indians from Kansas also are in attendance at Haskell, but most of them, except for the Potawatomis, attend the schools provided by the communities where they live.

The movement of the Indians to the new Indian Territory brought many missionary organizations to minister to their religious and educational needs. The Methodists, Presbyterians,

Baptists, Quakers, and Catholics sent their missionaries and teachers into the territory under the joint auspices of the government and the various churches. The government aided the missions in their educational work and thus permitted them to extend their religious activities among the Indians.

The Indian missions played a prominent part in the assimilation of the red men into the ways of the white men. There they were taught how to cultivate the soil and provide their own foods without dependence upon the Great White Father. The largest and most important of the missions, and also one of the earliest, was the Shawnee Mission, near Kansas City, established by Thomas Johnson for the Methodist Church. Some of its buildings are preserved by the state and various societies. The Presbyterian Mission at Highland is also well preserved and is housing an important collection of relics of an early day. The Baptist Mission to the Potawatomis, situated west of Topeka, can hardly be recognized today; the old mission building is now a barn. Nor did the Baptists preserve their mission to the Shawnees, to which the first printing press in Kansas was brought by Jotham Meeker, who undertook the publication of Indian material, the translation of religious tracts and songs into the Shawnee language, and the publication of a newspaper in that language. The Quaker mission to the Shawnees also has been lost, and the Catholic mission to the Osages no longer exists except in its location and in the preservation of many relics in St. Paul, Kansas.

3: *The First Christian Martyr of Kansas*

JUAN DE PADILLA, a Spanish Franciscan friar, who was chaplain to Coronado's little army when it came into Kansas in 1541, is presumed the first Christian martyr to die within the boundaries of the United States. He died in Kansas in 1542, according to tradition, on Christmas day.

Father Padilla had been a Spanish soldier before he became a priest, and much of his service in the ministry was with the armies. When Coronado began his long journey four priests accompanied the army of three hundred Spanish soldiers and about one thousand Indians and camp followers.

When the army arrived in what is now New Mexico and began visiting various Indian villages, the priests became missionaries to the Indian tribes. When Coronado and his band left winter quarters near the present town of Bernalillo, New Mexico, in the spring of 1541, Father Padilla was the only one available to accompany the troops to Kansas. There he became a missionary to the Indians, probably to the Pawnee tribe. He found the Indians exceptionally responsive to his teaching, and with them he built a huge wooden cross, which was set up at the end of the main street of the village. Under this cross Father Padilla read the masses of his church, converted and baptised the Indians, and performed other religious duties. In the meantime, Coronado and his men were exploring the neighborhood. They discovered that the stories told them of the riches owned by the Indians had been grossly exaggerated, were, in fact, pure myth.

Father Padilla is believed to have asked Coronado that he be allowed to spend the winter at Quivira. But he was denied permission and, being a good soldier, returned to the winter quarters at Tuguez with the army and remained there until the spring of 1542. Then he organized a little party, gathered up such supplies as were available in New Mexico, and set out for the Indian village whose inhabitants had been so receptive and apparently so eager to embrace Christianity and give up their pagan beliefs.

Coronado approved the decision and directed that the Indian guides who had accompanied the expedition from Quivira to the winter quarters return to their home with the friar. A Portuguese named Andres de Campo, an unnamed Negro, and two Indians from the Capotean tribe named Sebastian and Luke made up the little party. Coronado gave Father Padilla a horse, some sheep, mules, and ornaments to take with him to his new friends. The Spaniards then bade Father Padilla and his party Godspeed as they left for the north.

The journey to Quivira was made without incident, and the records disclose that much to Father Padilla's pleasure the cross was still standing at the head of the village street. A mission was erected, and Father Padilla began his work, which seems to have met with much success, for the entire tribe embraced the Catholic faith.

The Indians told the friar of another tribe living to the east of Quivira. These were the Guas, believed to be the Kaws, or Quas, as Coronado wrote the name of the tribe. The Quivira Indians warned the priest that the tribe was a treacherous one and advised him against trying to convert them to Christianity. But Father Padilla was determined to take his religion to the Guas. In his book *Quivira*, Paul Jones tells of the various theories about the circumstances leading to the martyrdom of Father Padilla:

A short distance farther [beyond the borders of Quivira] he was set upon by Indians who killed him. He had been warned by the Quivirans that it would be dangerous to proceed beyond their domain. When he saw the fate that awaited him he ordered his lay brothers to flee. As for himself, he knelt upon the prairie, his hands clasped before him and his eyes raised to heaven as the blow fell that crushed his skull.

There are a number of theories as to who killed Father Padilla and why. One of the narratives indicates that he was slain by his own lay brothers who coveted the horse, the mules, the sheep and the trinkets. Another narrative states that the Quivirans, having accepted his faith and feeling that they had gained thereby, were determined that its advantages should not be passed on to their enemies, the Guas. Therefore, they followed and killed him. Another theory, unsupported by the narratives, has it that the medicine men of the Kingdom of Quivira, jealous of the new religion, persuaded some of those who clung to the faith of their fathers to put the evangelist out of the way before the Indian gods should become offended and wreak vengeance on the tribe.[1]

The cities of Council Grove and Herington, thirty miles apart, each claim to be the site of Father Padilla's murder. The Quivira Historical Society erected a monument in Herington marking the spot where Padilla died. But the Council Grove monument to Coronado has the sounder claim as the actual site of the murder. It stands on the top of a rocky hill and can be seen for many miles east and west of the town. This rocky hill was noted in journals of early travelers along the Santa Fé trail.

According to the legends the two Indian laymen, Sebastian and Luke, were allowed to return to the spot where Father Padilla fell. They dug a shallow grave and after burying the priest piled a great cairn of rocks over the mound so that wild animals could not desecrate the grave.

When the Portuguese, Campo, and the Indians returned to Mexico after a long journey, a map of the area where the padre was killed was given to the Franciscan order, and a group of priests made the journey back to the site, found the cairn, placed the body in a coffin, and took it back to New Mexico, where

[1] Wichita, McCormick-Armstrong Company, 1929, 53–55.

it was buried in the chapel of the little mission church at Isleta.

The party of priests restored the cairn of stones after they removed the body of Father Padilla, and since the days of the Santa Fé Trail the cairn has been maintained by visitors and more recently by the citizens of Council Grove, who replace the stones carried away by souvenir hunters.

4: *The Shape We're In*

KANSAS is often referred to as a rectangle or "the grassy quadrangle" which sits astride the center of the continental United States and contains the greatest winter-wheat area in the world. It is a rectangle or parallelogram approximately four hundred miles long and two hundred miles wide. A look at the map seems to indicate that Kansas is a bit sway-backed. But that is the map's fault, because the parallels and meridians are marked to follow the curvature of the earth and are not straight lines.

It may be said that modern Kansas "isn't all there," since the state at one time comprised much more territory than it had when it was finally admitted to the Union. It had a grand opportunity to be still larger by taking in additional territory to the north. And it might have had a straight eastern border but for the fear some Missouri farmers had of the Indians.

The Missouri River forms the boundary of the northeastern corner of Kansas. When Missouri was admitted to the Union in 1821, the western boundary was approximately a straight line running north and south and crossing the Missouri River at the center of that stream and the center of the Kansas River where the two rivers join. That was the boundary for some years. This left a triangular area to the north and west of this river junction that included an area equivalent to about six counties and some extremely productive lands. The Iowas and the Sac and Foxes of Missouri were living in the area at the time, both small tribes and both willing and eager to embrace the white man's way of life. But the settlers who were moving into Missouri or westward to larger or better farms were afraid of them and began agitating for their removal. They pointed out that the settlers who lived south of the Missouri River were protected from the Osage Indians by the creation of a neutral strip thirty miles wide between the western boundary of that state and the new Osage reservation.

The new settlers suggested that the Missouri River itself would be a sufficient natural barrier against hypothetical raiding Indians. So by the Platte Purchase in 1836 the government bought the lands of the Iowas and the Sac and Fox tribes of Missouri. The Iowas were moved directly across the river into Kansas, and the Sac and Fox Indians were given a reservation just south of the one allotted to the Iowas.

The lands thus secured and opened to settlement were annexed to Missouri. That is how Kansas lost that nick out of the northeastern corner. But it happened long before Kansas was thought of as a territory, in fact, before it was even designated as the territory to which the tribes from New York and the Northwest Territory were to be moved. Moreover, it is generally recognized that the river forms a natural boundary between the two states. Yet the use of the Missouri River as a boundary has brought about several problems. There is an entire school district belonging to Kansas on the east side of the river. Many tracts of land belonging to Kansas have been found to be in Missouri and vice versa, as the result of the wanderlust of the Missouri River. Only in 1949 did the two states finally settle their boundary problems along the river in a compact approved by both legislatures whereby Missouri lands found in Kansas were ceded to Kansas and Kansas lands found in Missouri were ceded to Missouri, with the exception of that school district. It still belongs to Kansas.

How It Started

The southern boundary of Kansas is the thirty-seventh parallel; the northern boundary is the fortieth parallel. There was comparatively little difficulty in fixing these lines. The question arose in Congress whether or not the southern boundary should be an extension of the southern boundary of Missouri, but a final agreement was reached placing the Kansas boundary at the thirty-seventh parallel, thus giving additional land to the newly formed Indian Territory.

The northern border was the subject of a long debate in the Wyandotte Constitutional Convention of 1859. Nebraska and Kansas had previously been made territories at the same time. Kansas was the battleground over the slavery question, and the territory made more rapid progress in settlement than its neighbor. When Kansas had won, by the force of an overwhelming vote, the right to abolish slavery, it was generally conceded that Kansas would soon become a state. The people of Nebraska living south of the Platte River wanted to become a part of that state. They had no idea that Nebraska was likely to become a state within a few years. Hence, when an election to select delegates to the Wyandotte Convention was called, the Nebraskans also sent a panel of representatives.

The delegates were on hand when the convention met. But since Kansas did not know what was going on in the territory to the north, Nebraska had not been included in the call, and the convention declined to seat the delegation. However, when the time came to settle the northern boundary, the Nebraska men were allowed to join in the debate and argue their case before the convention.

The Nebraska men offered the same reason for including their area with Kansas as had been offered in the making of the Platte Purchase in Missouri. The Platte River was a wide stream, they said, with low banks which made it subject to overflow. The channel of the stream has great quantities of quicksand, and it is a dangerous stream to cross much of the time. Because of the nature of the stream bed and the vagaries of the river, the Nebraskans told the convention it was practically impossible to bridge the Platte. Thus the river would furnish a natural barrier against the Indians from the northern plains, who were at that time untamed and considered dangerous by the white settlers.

But the Nebraska proposal was not accepted. One reason advanced for turning down the Nebraskans was that there might be difficulties over the capital of the state. Another was the expressed fear of several Republicans that annexation of the Nebraska area would give the Democrats control over the first state legislature. The convention determined not to include the area with Kansas under the new constitution. Then an effort was made to adopt a resolution to request Congress to include that portion of Nebraska south of the Platte with Kansas when the bill approving the Wyandotte Constitution was adopted, but this proposal also failed by a substantial vote, and the northern boundary was established at the fortieth parallel.

The question of the western boundary of Kansas also caused long debate in the Wyandotte Convention. The act by which the Kansas Territory was created had provided that the southern boundary extend along the thirty-seventh parallel as far west as the state of New Mexico, then north to the thirty-eighth parallel and west on that line to the summit of the Rocky Mountains, then north at the Continental Divide to the fortieth parallel and east to the Missouri River.

The western boundary disputes helped to give western Kansas a bad name from the very beginning, when members of the convention who had never seen the area declared the high prairies to be fit habitations only for prairie dogs, owls, buffalo, and rattlesnakes, making this assumption from the journals of Lieutenant Pike and Major Long. Horace Greeley, in his trips across the country, also found little to become excited about in the region and wrote to the *New York Tribune* most disparagingly concerning it. So it wasn't any wonder that the men who made up the personnel of the constitutional convention thought that the new state should not be burdened with a lot of territory which they believed had no value.

There were some members of the convention who wanted to make Kansas a square state. They would fix the western boundary at the sixth meridian and give all the rest of present Kansas and eastern Colorado back to the Indians. They wanted a state small and compact in area, with uniform climate and soil, which would result in a general similarity of life and occupation for its inhabitants. There was another group which was willing to go a bit farther westward, but only to provide large ranchlands for the cattle they felt might be needed to fit in with the program of a balanced agriculture for the crop-producing sections to the east.

Gold had just been discovered in the Colorado Mountains, and miners were flocking across Kansas to the new fields. Members of the convention had seen these miners and their friends and didn't like their appearance. They felt the miners were more than a trifle rough and their life incompatible with that of the farmers of Kansas. Also, some members of the convention had heard about the life led by the cattle barons of Texas, a life they did not feel would fit into the ideal picture of a homogeneous citizenry they hoped to create.

"It is simply a question of how far west this section of country can be inhabited—how far there is timber, water, and grass," said W. Hutchinson, a member from Douglas County.

Solon O. Thacher, also from Douglas County, remarked that a large portion of the western region was "a miserable, uninhabited region." J. J. Blunt of Anderson urged that the western boundary be no farther west than near where Hays now stands. "We would then embrace all of the desirable territory upon this side of that large, sterile plain," he said.

B. Wrigley of Doniphan pointed out that west of the twenty-third or the twenty-fourth meridians there was "an expanse of territory of equal width and of equal extent, barren, sterile, and unfit for agricultural purposes." He urged that there would be diversity of interests between the eastern and western portions of the new state that could cause difficulties later. "I believe," he said, "these two interests are incompatible; that this sterile plain which intervenes between the agricultural and mineral portions of Kansas is so wide, occupied only by wild animals and unfit for cultivation to such an extent as to render the community of interests altogether incompatible."

The western boundary was finally fixed at the twenty-fifth meridan west from Washington, D. C. Kansas thus gave up a large section of the High Plains area and the eastern side of the mountains, where there were great coal and mineral deposits. It also lost Denver, which was founded in Arapahoe County, Kansas, by a group of Kansas men and was named for one of the territorial governors of Kansas.

It may be noted here that the Kansas boundary as shown on many maps does not conform to the line fixed by the convention at Wyandotte and approved by the United States Congress. This is the result of the use of different meridians. Many map makers use the Greenwich meridian as a base. The Capitol at Washington is situated on the seventy-seventh meridian west of Greenwich, England. But Congress had decreed that measurements in the United States should be made with the first meridian as the base line. The naval observatory in Washington, D. C. was to be the base. The result is a decrepancy of three minutes and six seconds between the one hundred and second and the twenty-fifth meridians. At the thirty-eighth parellel this amounts to 2.81 miles. Thus, at the crossing of the Arkansas River, the western boundary of Kansas will be found to be 2.81 miles west of the one hundred and second meridian west of Greenwich and on the twenty-fifth meridian west of Washington.

When Kansas was formed into a territory in 1854, it comprised 126,283 square miles. When the Wyandotte Constitutional Convention of 1859 concluded its work and the state was admitted to the Union in 1861, the area of the state was put at 81,318 square miles, only a slight difference from the latest census figure, which shows 81,774 square miles within those boundaries.

5: *They Spelled It by Ear*

THE NAME of the fair state of Kansas has had some unusual, not to say wonderful, spellings. It seems that a good many of the early visitors to Kansas must have spelled the name of the Indian tribe from which the state got its name either by ear or by guess and by golly. If you don't believe it, take a look at the fifty-four different ways of spelling the name of the Indian tribe without spelling it as it appears in the histories, geographies, and other printed material of the present day.

The earliest visitors were Spaniards. After them a considerable number of French traders, explorers, and later colonial Americans and explorers came out to collect furs, see the country, and perhaps make a fortune.

Many of these early travelers kept diaries or journals and tried to record faithfully the events of their travels and something about the Indian tribes they visited or heard about. As they wrote these journals or diaries during the course of their travels, or when they returned home and dictated their stories to a friend or an employed amanuensis, they tried to translate into the Spanish, French, or English syllables the curious expressions of the Indians who tried to tell the "foreigner" who they were and to what tribe they belonged. The results were some fearful spellings of the name Kansas. Just how these visitors could get so many variations of the same word is beyond the ken of the historians and linguists who were consulted for what light they could throw on the various spellings and pronunciations.

Here are the fifty-five ways of spelling the name of the "Sunflower State":

Acansis	Canze	Kans	Kants	Kauzaus
Akansa	Canzes	Kansa	Kanzan	Kaw
Canceas	Canzon	Kansae	Kanzas	Kaws
Cancez	Caugh	Kansas	Kanzes	Konza
Canchez	Caw	Kansaws	Kanzon	Konzas
Canips	Chanzes	Kanse	Karsea	Konzo
Cansa	Ka Anjou	Kansea	Kasas	Okams
Canses	Kah	Kanses	Kase	Okanis
Cansez	Kamse	Kansez	Kathagi	Quaus
Canzan	Kances	Kansies	Kaus	Ukasa
Canzas	Kanees	Kantha	Kausau	Ukasak

There is grave doubt whether the present spelling is the correct one. As near as can be ascertained, the Indians pronounced the name of the tribe in two syllables. The French seem to be farther away from both the spelling and the pronunciation of the word than either the Spanish or the English explorers and trappers who wandered through the region. Rev. Isaac McCoy translated the name of the tribe early in the nineteenth century into Kausau. Edward Everett Hale, the well-known Boston divine and active leader of the abolitionists, wrote the first book about the territories of Kansas and Nebraska.[1] He devoted an entire chapter to the origin of the name but spelled it throughout as Kanzas and insisted that the people of the state would finally adopt that spelling. In the journal of the Lewis and Clark expedition the name of the tribe is spelled six different ways, including the present spelling. The government began to adopt the present spelling as early as 1815, when it made a treaty with the tribe.

The present legal spelling of the name of the state may easily have been the result of an error by either a writer or a printer, since in some chirography it is difficult to distinguish a "U"

[1] *Kansas and Nebraska* (Boston, Phillips, 1854).

QUIVIRA
JUAN DE
PADILLA
MARTYR
FOR THE
FAITH
YIELDED HIS LIFE
HERE IN 1542

CORONADO 1541
J. V. BROWER 1896
ERECTED BY
ROBERT HENDERSON
C. R. SCHILLING
AND
REV. J. F. LEARY
FOR
QUIVIRA
HISTORICAL
SOCIETY
1904
KANSAS U.S.A.

O. H. S.

Monument of the site of the murder of Juan de Padilla

from an "N," and many persons make similar marks for the letters "S" and "Z." In a number of the early journals, which the Kansas Historical Society now owns, there are several spellings of the Indian tribe which experts are unable to decipher. The name Kaw, as applied to the Indian tribe now living in Oklahoma and to the major river in Kansas, is a modern abbreviation which probably originated in Pike's journal, where it is spelled "Kaus." Incidentally, should the remnants of this tribe disappear, there would be no legal geographical designation of the name Kaw in Kansas. The statute books recognize the name of the river only as the Kansas River.

There is also quite a difference of opinion about the meaning of the name. In some of the early books Kansas is said to mean "smoky" or "hazy." A traveler visiting the area in October or early November might agree to this interpretation. Other writers, however, have said that the name means "windy" and that the Kaw Indians were the "People of the South Wind." Still another group asserted that the name means "swift river" or "swift water." All of these interpretations may be applied to Kansas. But the enduring interpretation of the name will never be written in small numbers of words.

6: *The Kansas Melting Pot*

THE SETTLEMENT of Kansas assumed a different pattern from the common one. Most frontier areas witnessed the infiltration of persons and property at a gradual pace as the forward movement of civilization slowly pushed the wilderness ahead. Kansas, however, was settled by mass migrations that came sporadically. At first these migrations were the result of the bitter struggle over slavery; later they were produced by the immigration of foreign peoples.

It should be remembered that from about 1825 until the opening of Kansas Territory in 1854, Kansas was a part of the Indian Territory, originally a vast area consisting of the major portion of the Louisiana Purchase. Then came the slavery issue, the abrogation of the Missouri Compromise, and the establishment of the doctrine of "Squatter Sovereignty," which brought about the organization of Kansas Territory in 1854 and the first migrations.

Taken by themselves, the reports of the explorers who saw no value in the territory likely would have caused settlement of Kansas to assume orthodox proportions. But when it was decreed that the destiny of Kansas lay in the expression of its people about slavery, the supporters of both sides of the issue sought to assure that their side would win by predominance of votes; hence the influx of settlers prior to the Civil War.

The census taken in Kansas in 1860 shows more residents from Missouri than from any other state. At that time Missouri was predominantly southern in its attitude toward the slavery question. To counter this situation, the New England Emigrant Aid Society organized great groups of northerners to settle in Kansas. Jim Lane made a barnstorming tour through Illinois, Indiana, Ohio, and Michigan, which resulted in the organization of what became known as "Lane's Army." His pleading influenced a great number of men and some women to come to Kansas, to find a home as an incidental purpose and to carry out a militant assault upon slavery as the main goal.

The South was no less diligent in seeking settlers for Kansas. Several societies were organized in Georgia and Alabama with branches in other states. The Alabama colony sent almost as many southern settlers as the New England Emigrant Aid Society did. The caprices of Kansas climate broke up the southern movement, however, and those who had succumbed to the earlier lure generally returned home soon after experiencing one season of the cutting winds and biting cold of winter or the hot, dry winds of summer.

How It Started

In *People of Kansas*[1] it is pointed out that the census of 1860 shows the birthplaces of the inhabitants to be well scattered over the northern states, with the majority in Missouri, Illinois, Ohio, and Indiana. In subsequent census periods Missouri and Illinois were shown to have furnished the bulk of Kansas population.

Following the Civil War and the enactment of the Homestead Act, which gave free lands to Union soldiers, there came another mass migration to Kansas. In 1872 and 1873, the Land Office records show that 16,000 persons proved up on their claims, the larger proportion having claims in Kansas. Also about this same time the large movements of foreign-born began. The first of these new settlers were the Swedes. Because of a terrific drouth on the Scandinavian Peninsula, thousands were forced to move to other lands, and early reports by the more venturesome dubbed Kansas the land of opportunity. Various Swedish societies were formed to help bring the refugees to America and settle them in Minnesota and Kansas, and the Kansas Pacific Railroad offered great tracts of lands to them.

The second large foreign group to come to Kansas was a Mennonite colony of German origin which settled in Marion, McPherson, Reno, Harvey, and Butler counties in 1874 and succeeding years. This strongly religious group immigrated in numbers which have never been exceeded by any other national group in Kansas. The original colony was made up of two masses. One of these came directly from Germany, the other from Germany by way of Russia, where their ancestors had gone one hundred years before. Both migrant groups came to the United States to seek freedom of religion and education, to achieve local self-government, and to be free from the prevailing European requirement for bearing arms. Catherine the Great instigated the treaty with an earlier generation of Mennonites in order to persuade hardy and thrifty farmers to move

[1] By Carroll D. Clark and Roy L. Roberts (Topeka, Kansas State Planning Board, 1936).

into the Crimea, which she had recently wrested from Turkey. She guaranteed everything the Mennonites asked, and many accepted the offer.

The Russian treaty had another effect, however. The Prussian government saw in its terms the possibility of a great emigration of its best farmers and made a counteroffer containing the same guarantees of freedom to those who would remain on their lands. Therefore many remained, and when the treaty was about to expire the Russians granted the Mennonites the right to migrate to whatever country they chose and simultaneously made a treaty with Germany which provided that the German Mennonites would be allowed to accompany their brethren to any country. The result was a large migration of Russian and German Mennonites, who settled on Santa Fé Railroad lands and some government lands in central Kansas.

The next movement of foreign-born was that of the Russian-German population which moved into Ellis, Rush, Russell, and adjoining counties. These people of German origin had gone to Russia from southern Germany under the same type of treaty which Catherine had made with the Mennonites. They were mainly Roman Catholics who settled along the Don and Volga rivers to the north and east of the Mennonite settlements. Their treaty expired at approximately the same time as the first; they could either return to Germany or choose a new country. Most of them chose America, and the regions where they settled reveal many of their old world traditions.

There were three important British colonies in Kansas, only one of which obtained permanent status in the state and was assimilated to its mode of life. This group colonized at Wakefield, in Clay County, and was chiefly a farming community composed of settlers from England and Scotland who came to America to grow up with the country. At both Victoria and Runnymede, the colonists were of the landed gentry, a class of British more noted for riding to hounds and enjoying the pleasures of their estates than for possessing the hardihood necessary to the settlement and cultivation of a frontier. Only a few of these colonists remained to adapt their lives to the Kansas pattern.

There were, in addition, hundreds of British subjects who came to Kansas from 1880 to 1900, but these came in small family groups, purchased farms, or went into business or industry. Family groups of Bohemians also arrived, to settle in Republic, Cloud, and near-by counties. Several small colonies of Frenchmen came to Kansas, too. One group settled in Cloud County and another in Franklin County. The Franklin group was organized on a co-operative community basis, but the plan failed and many moved away. The French who came to northern Kansas, however, were chiefly farmers who remained, merged their way of life with that of their new home, and are now an important segment of Kansas life.

Then there were Danes and Norwegians, some Dutch and Canadians, and not a few Welsh and Irish who settled in Kansas. But no discussion of the mass migrations would be even reasonably complete without mention of the "Exodus," the great surge of Negroes who came to a free Kansas from the end of the Civil War through the seventies. Thousands of Negroes moved northward, chiefly on foot, to the banks of the Mississippi or to the rail lines leading toward Kansas. They had no money and few clothes. They were fed by citizens along their route, who also purchased boat fare for them. For many the trip to Kansas required months. In some instances communities chartered steamers to transport the migrants. Railroads allowed the Negroes to travel free in boxcars, and hundreds came by this means into the southern part of the state, where they were dumped out of the cars as soon as the border was crossed. In Kansas, the cities of Kansas City, Topeka, and Parsons raised considerable sums to care for these destitute people, and for some months the Santa Fé Railroad provided a barracks in its shops in Topeka. There was a tragic period of want for many before they were finally settled in shacks.

From Kentucky came the well-known Nicodemus Colony, which purchased an entire township in Graham County and settled it with Negroes from that state. This group had sufficient money to obtain the lands and to farm them, and the colony always has been as prosperous as the vagaries of plains climate will permit.

It is a curious anomaly, as Carl Becker noted in his essay, *Kansas,* published in 1910, that out of these diverse currents of migration, native and foreign, should have come not only the state of Kansas but that state of mind which makes the savannahs of the east and the vast prairie of the west a place to which allegiance is sworn.

It was not a region for those who feared space, for the limitless land met the limitless sky at the edge of the world, and over it all was a sunny silence. "Dear old Kansas!" Becker heard a young girl exclaim as her train brought her back once more to the miles of corn fields and the thin line of sunflowers along the right of way. This was home. And so it was for those earlier peoples who found in the soil of Kansas the source of a new culture.

7: *Battle Lines Are Drawn*

EVER SINCE the enactment by the United States Congress of the Missouri Compromise, in which it was decreed that slave-holding should not be permitted north of the thirty-eighth parallel except in Missouri, the struggle for power between the slavery and antislavery forces in the country had grown. Both sides recognized that the increasing population and the need for additional lands for settlement must necessarily bring additional states into the Union. Texas would not allow itself to be split into several states, and only the areas comprising New Mexico and Arizona could be brought into the Union as slave states under the Missouri Compromise. It was evident in the South that the antislave states would soon hold the balance of power in the Senate, which would enable them to outvote the South. The doctrine of squatter sovereignty seemed to offer a way out. Yet in the very first trial of the doctrine the proslavery forces took a beating that helped to precipitate the Civil War.

Kansas was the center of this catastrophic contest. Both sides were fully organized, and both sides were determined. The result was five years of internecine strife in Kansas, followed by four years of bloody warfare between the North and the South.

Originally the New England Emigrant Aid Society was not a charitable organization but hoped to make substantial profits from handling the business of prospective settlers in Kansas. The society began moving emigrants into Kansas in the late summer and fall of 1854 and continued its activities until the battle was won. From the South the largest organized colonies were those of Colonel Buford and the Alabama groups. But, as has been said, a single winter in Kansas was too rough for settlers from the deep South, and most of them returned to their homes. However, the Missourians and some of the more rugged individuals from northern sections of the South, did not succumb to the rigorous climate.

The events leading to this change in the society's stature began when the Missourians moved into the new territory in such substantial numbers for the first elections in 1855 that they controlled the ballots and elected most of the members of the two branches of the territorial legislature. When the legislature met at Pawnee, the proslavery representatives proceeded to throw out most of the abolitionists in the legislature on the ground that they had been elected by fraud. The legislature then proceeded to move from Pawnee to the Shawnee Mission, where it virtually enacted the Missouri statute book, changing

35

only the name of the state. In the statutes dealing with slavery, the legislature legalized slave-holding and established the death penalty for interference with slaves or slaveowners.

The men who had come into the territory from the North fought fire with fire. John Brown, C. R. Jennison, James Montgomery, and James H. Lane (later United States senator), conducted active campaigns against the Missouri marauders. Their cohorts conducted raids into Missouri to carry off slaves and other property, while the Missourians came into Kansas and intimidated, threatened, and sometimes robbed and killed the new abolitionist settlers. There were many pitched battles between the warring elements.

During the territorial years in Kansas there were nine different governors who came to the state pledged to honest government but who were recalled or dismissed when they did not give the proslavery factions preference in every activity.

James H. Lane and John Brown went during these years to the eastern states to tell the people about conditions in Kansas. Their efforts so aroused the people that large sums of money were collected to aid in the campaign, and, with the aid of the New England organization, thousands of men were recruited to take an active part in the settlement of Kansas and the fighting incident to its admission into the Union as an abolitionist state. In retaliation the Missourians stopped the usual modes of transportation, rail, wagon, horseback, and steamboat. Hence the Lane Trail was organized across Iowa, starting at the railhead at Iowa City, proceeding to Nebraska City, Nebraska, across the Missouri River, and from there south to Topeka. Iowa citizens erected stone cairns along the trail so that travelers would not become lost.

From Topeka the new settlers were sent to near-by communities to take claims and become bona fide settlers and citizens. In the meantime there were several raids by the Missouri folk who sacked Lawrence, robbed new homes, committed murder, and destroyed free-state newspaper plants.

Three unsuccessful constitutions were written for Kansas before one was finally accepted by Congress. The first one was written at Topeka in October, 1855, after the call for a constitutional convention by a gathering of free-state men at Big Springs. Jim Lane was the chairman of the Kansas executive committee, which promoted the Topeka convention and the election sponsored by it. It was pointed out that California had called its own constitutional convention without waiting for congressional authority and had drafted a constitution which Congress accepted. There seemed to be a possibility that Congress might accept a constitution written and approved by the people of Kansas.

The Topeka constitution was thoroughly opposed to slavery. It was written within a period of three weeks, after which the Kansas executive committee called an election. The proslavery residents of the territory did not vote in this election; therefore, the constitution was adopted all but unanimously. Then another election was called and a complete slate of state officers, with Dr. Charles Robinson as governor, and a legislature were elected. Again the proslavery faction did not vote. But when the legislature attempted to meet, it was opposed by a company of United States dragoons under specific instructions from Jefferson Davis, secretary of war of the United States, and later president of the Confederacy, to stop the session. The commander of the troops had deployed them around the city and went alone to the senate and house chambers. He explained that he had a distasteful task but that he was under orders to prevent the legislative session. The legislators accepted the directive from the army and dispersed without any show of resistance. Some hotheads urged that the legislature meet in defiance of the army orders, but the majority counseled obedience to the order.

The second constitution was written at Lecompton, then the capital of the Territory, in 1857. This constitution sought to retain the slave-holding rights with limitations but in other respects was similar to the Topeka constitution. In an effort to persuade the people of Kansas to adopt the Lecompton constitution Congress passed the English Bill, which granted Kansas large land acreages for a common-school endowment. The vote for adoption on December 21, 1857, was favorable but indicated that the antislavery faction had not been allowed to participate in some districts. In those areas where the abolitionists did vote, the constitution was rejected. In a subsequent election on the constitution called by Acting Governor Frederick P. Stanton, January 4, 1858, the free-staters rejected the Lecompton Constitution by a vote of 10,288 to 138, thus reversing the previous result in the December election. But this was not enough, for Congress referred the Lecompton Constitution back to the people of Kansas once more, and in the third election on it, August 2, 1858, they voted 11,812 to 1,926 against!

The third constitutional convention was to be held in Minneola, a town as yet only projected on paper, but which had been widely promoted. When the delegates assembled there, they could find no satisfactory meeting place and no hotels or even reasonably adequate housing. Further, it was discovered that members of the legislature who had voted for the convention to meet there also held title to business and residential lots in the proposed town. The Minneola "swindle" blew up in the faces of the promoters on the first day of the convention, and the delegates voted to transfer the convention to Leavenworth immediately. Minneola faded from prominence directly thereafter, and the highly colored lithographs showing the town plat and the great public buildings were destined to become museum pieces. The Leavenworth constitution, a wishy-washy document which neither side considered adequate or satisfactory, was adopted by the voters May 18, 1858, but rejected by Congress.

The fourth constitution was written at Wyandotte (later a section of Kansas City, Kansas) after the enactment of the

Peace Act, or Amnesty Law, by the territorial legislature in 1859. This act provided that all political prisoners should be released, that all charges against alleged political criminals should be dismissed, and that both sides should have complete freedom to vote in the election.

The result of the convention was determined when the delegates were elected: the abolitionists had moved into the territory in such numbers that their slate of delegates was elected in most of the districts. Too, it had been agreed by the leaders of both the abolition and slavery factions that those who had been active on either side in the earlier election campaigns or who had worked on the three earlier constitutions should not be sent to the Wyandotte convention as delegates.

The convention, after assembling July 5, 1859, wrote the constitution (under which, modified by amendments, Kansas still functions) in twenty-nine days. By it, slavery was prohibited in the new state. When the constitution was adopted by the people, an election was held as provided for, and a full slate of state officers and representatives to the national legislature were chosen more than a year before Congress voted statehood for the territory. The election of Lincoln to the presidency in 1860 foretold the early admission of Kansas into the Union as a free state. The House of Representatives had already approved the constitution, but the Senate delayed action until Congress met after the elections.

The South held the balance of power in the Senate, and it was not until some of the southern senators had withdrawn and declared for secession that there was an actual majority in the Senate favorable to the Kansas constitution. The bill for statehood was passed late in January, and on January 29, 1861, President James Buchanan issued the proclamation admitting Kansas to the Union as the thirty-fourth state. The state government began operations on February 9; the state legislature convened in March. Directly thereafter came the attack on Fort Sumter and the call for volunteers for the Union Army.

For the most part, Kansas lands were spared during the Civil War period, except for Quantrill's vicious raid on Lawrence. During the war Kansas was asked for a quota of sixteen thousand men for the Union armies. Actually, the state furnished over twenty thousand men, the largest number of active soldiers in the Union Army from any state, in proportion to population. It should be noted, however, that a large number of men enrolled in Kansas regiments had joined outfits quartered near their homes and never set foot on Kansas soil until after the war ended.

For Kansas, the worst period of the war came late in 1864, when General Sterling Price and his Confederate armies swept across Missouri toward Fort Leavenworth with the avowed purpose of securing the vast military stores at the post, which had been accumulated for the Army of the Border. The army had comparatively few men at Fort Leavenworth and near-by camps—about four thousand in all. Governor Thomas Carney of Kansas issued a call for all males from sixteen to sixty years of age to enlist in the militia. It was a motley army thus recruited. The men were armed with rifles, shotguns, or clubs, and some had no weapons of any kind. Nearly seventeen thousand old men and boys were enrolled in the various regiments. They furnished their own transportation, clothing, cooking utensils, bedding, and tents. The army provided the food.

These civilian soldiers, together with trained army men, met General Price in the battles of the Little Blue, the Big Blue, and Westport. All these engagements took place in Missouri, near the Kansas line. The militia turned back the southern forces and later engaged a contingent of Price's armies in the Battle of Mine Run, the battle which involved the largest number of soldiers ever to fight on Kansas soil. The Confederate soldiers were driven out of Kansas with severe losses, while the Kansas militia suffered comparatively few casualties. Some of the militia regiments were sent to Fort Riley to guard against possible Indian attacks, and other units were stationed along the border between Missouri and Kansas to guard against any flanking movement by Price. The militia served only seventeen days, after which time the men were mustered out of service and returned home.

THIS PLACE CALLED KANSAS:

II.   *How It Grew*

Colonel S. N. Wood

8: *Once the Town Boomer's Paradise*

URING at least two periods in the history of Kansas the state was inhabited by a most aggressive group of town boomers. There are town boomers, and there are honest town boomers. Both types operated in Kansas in the early days and again in the boom period of the eighties. Apart from the fact that the boomers of the later period were a bit more suave, there was little difference between their methods and the blatant efforts of the boomers of territorial and early statehood days.

The boomers of the early period seemed to be trying to establish towns on the corners of every section in the eastern townships. In the later period they moved into western Kansas, and, in addition to promoting towns, engaged in some of the riotous quarrels over the selection of county seats. In fact, most of the county-seat conflicts, some of which led to bloodshed, were brought about by town promoters who sold lots to citizens on the promise that their town would certainly be selected as the county seat. The town that lost out was like the Arab who "folded his tent and silently stole away."

In the earliest days, fourteen cities were promoted on the Kansas side of the Missouri River. Now only three towns and a village or two may be found along the river. Kansas City, Leavenworth, and Atchison are the important cities along the river, although their glory as river terminals faded when the river steamboats gave up the long fight against sand bars, snags, and inadequate navigation aids.

One of the towns expected to be important among the river terminals was Sumner, which was situated a few miles downstream from Atchison and was the first Kansas home of John J. Ingalls, the prominent lawyer, author, statesman, and orator. Ingalls came to Sumner from Massachusetts in the fall of 1858, having been "sold" by a map and a prospectus which depicted the town as unusually prosperous and growing. Shortly after his arrival Ingalls wrote his father as follows:

That chromatic triumph of lithographed mendacity, supplemented by the loquacious embellishments of a lively adventurer who has been laying out townsites and staking off corner lots for some years past at Topeka, exhibited a scene in which the attractions of art, nature, science, commerce and religion were artistically blended. Innumerable drays were transporting from a fleet of gorgeous steamboats vast cargoes of foreign and domestic merchandise over Russ pavements to collosal warehouses of brick and stone. Dense, wide streets of elegant residences rose with gentle ascent from the shores of the tranquil stream. Numerous parks, decorated with rare trees, shrubbery and fountains, were surrounded with the mansions of the great and the temples of their devotion. The adjacent eminences were crowned with costly piles which wealth, directed by intelligence and controlled by taste, had erected for the education of the rising generation of Sumnerites. The only shadow upon the enchanting landscape fell from the clouds of smoke that poured from the towering shafts of her acres of manufactories, which the whole circumference of the undulating prairie was white with endless, sinuous trains of wagons slowly moving toward the mysterious regions of Farther West.[1]

[1] From the John J. Ingalls Clippings (Topeka, Kansas State Historical Society).

It was at Sumner that Ingalls met Jonathan Gardener Lang, a jug fisherman, melon raiser, truck gardener, and habitual drunkard. Ingalls often went out in a boat with Lang when he was running his jug lines in the river. Later Ingalls wrote "Catfish Aristocracy,"[2] a carefully prepared description of those who live somewhat precariously in shanty towns along important rivers. Lang was told that he ought to sue Ingalls, but Ingalls appeased the fisherman with a sack of flour and a slab of bacon. Sumner practically disappeared in 1860 when a tornado destroyed a considerable part of the town.

Indianola was laid out a few miles northwest of Topeka and for some years was a much larger town than Topeka. Situated at the point where the military road from Fort Leavenworth to Fort Riley came down from the hills and crossed Soldier Creek, Indianola had substantial store buildings and many frame residences by the time the Kansas Pacific Railroad was projected in the Kaw River valley. The men who owned the townsite were asked to vote bonds and donate lands for a right of way for the railroad. They did neither, and the railroad was built to Eugene, now North Topeka and missed Indianola by four miles. As a result, Indianola soon languished and faded away.

Kansas has lost about six thousand geographical designations in the almost one hundred years of her history as an organized commonwealth. Of course, some of these geographic names are of rivers and of counties and townships where names were changed frequently to satisfy the whims of individuals or groups who might have influence in the legislature. An example of this may be noted in the story of Grasshopper Falls and the Grasshopper River, in northeastern Kansas. The people living in the town and along the river didn't relish the name and for some years protested violently and demanded a change. Finally the state legislature agreed to change the name of the town to Sautrelle Falls and the river to the Sautrelle. Some jester in the

[2] *Kansas Magazine*, Vol. I (1872).

legislature had a good many chuckles in substituting the French word for grasshopper in the names. The citizens were more up in arms than ever when they discovered what the legislature had done and at the next session they acted in earnest, informed the legislators that if they had to have the name Grasshopper, they wanted the good old American word and not some French version. They finally got their way; the town's name was changed to Valley Falls, and the River was renamed the Delaware.

James G. Sands, a pioneer of Lawrence, described the ease with which a town could be organized:

During 1855, 1856, and 1857, interests in towns, consisting of twelve lots, circulated as freely as the "wild cat" currency of that period. Lithographs, showing beautiful parks, with fountains playing, band stands, ornamental trees and shrubbery surrounding magnificent public buildings, beckoned onward the "tenderfoot" to fortune who never had speculation in his eye before.

In 1857 a convivial party of gentlemen had gathered at the Eldridge House, Lawrence, when the suggestion was made that before they separate they lay out a town. In the party were several surveyors, who at once proceeded to make the proper drawings; a fine lithograph was procured and the blank space filled in, which completed the certificate of the birth of Oread.

These are the incidents that gave life for a brief period to one of the many towns that sprung into existence by the motion of a pen. Shares were put on the market and sold like hot cakes at prices of ten to fifty dollars a share. I was the happy owner of one of these but before the crisis came I unloaded my interest.[3]

It should be pointed out that the town was planned in Lawrence and then the promoters went looking for a site. Oread was finally located in Coffey County, about twelve miles northeast of Burlington.

The later promotion activities in Kansas, during the boom

[3] From the *Collections* of the Kansas Historical Society (1911–12), 432.

48

days of the eighties, resulted in the loss of many thousands of dollars when towns were overbuilt with business houses and residences for settlers who never arrived.

A classic story of the boom days in Wichita concerned a man from Iowa who had seen some of the press-agent material about Wichita in the heyday of its boom. The Iowan went to Wichita and looked the town over. He saw a likely business lot at a corner about a mile from the center of town. It was offered to him for $10,000 by a real-estate agent representing a man who had bought the lot a week earlier for $8,000. The Iowan said he would think it over until morning. When he went to the agent's office the next morning the lot had been sold, and workmen were already excavating for a bank and office building. The Iowan went two blocks west and bought a corner lot for $10,000 and then returned to Iowa to await an offer of $25,000 for the property. The offer never came, the boom "busted" in a few months, and about fifty years ago the lot adjoining the one owned by the Iowan was sold for $300. The Iowan held to his lot, refusing to consider any offer less than $10,000. He kept the taxes paid, and his estate sold the lot sixty years after its purchase for one-fourth the original price.

The town of Rome was founded in 1867 in present Ellis County. W. E. ("Buffalo Bill") Cody erected the first stone building on the townsite. Within a year after its founding Rome had a population of two thousand, a curious hodgepodge of citizens, as one writer put it, typical of that always found in frontier towns: businessmen, soldiers, railroad graders, gamblers, hunters, cutthroats, and prostitutes. Numerically, saloons were in the ascendancy among business establishments. In that same year Fort Hays was established. The railroad built a heavy grade to lift the tracks from the floodwaters of a near-by creek, and the town of Hays was founded. Rome was cut off from the post by the high railroad grade, and within a year or so it, too, faded away.

The towns of Runnymede and Victoria, while far apart,

were similar in many respects. Both were colonies established by English people. Runnymede, in Harper County, was intended to be a co-operative colony, but the combination of weather and farm life proved too much for the colonists, who soon returned to their old homes and abandoned Runnymede to the prairies. Victoria is still on the map, but most of the English who settled the original town and brought in fine cattle and horses were discouraged by the death of the promoter and soon moved away. This group had built a dam across a creek and provided a steam yacht for summer evening recreation. One day a big rain washed out the dam, and the yacht mired in the mud many miles down the Smoky Hill River. One legend claims that the engine was later used in a sawmill at Ellsworth. Another claims it furnished the power for a newspaper plant. The English settlers never attempted to recover their yacht.

A good many of the boom towns disappeared when the booms "busted," and in the first half of the twentieth century Kansas lost more than half its towns, villages, and post offices as a result of the development of rural free delivery and the increasing use of the motor car, airplane, and truck on farms. A trip to the county seat to pay taxes and make purchases was an all-day affair in the horse-and-buggy days; now it is only a matter of minutes. It is reasonable to assume that we have not seen the last of the Kansas town failures as these same forces continue to effect their changes.

9: *Bogus Counties and Bogus Bonds*

IN THE early eighteen seventies Kansas broke out in a rash of fraudulent counties, cities, and school districts. Just how much these frauds cost the residents of the various communities will never be known. For example, only in 1946 did Comanche County make final payments in the last re-funding of bogus bonds issued by the forgers in 1873.

Many of the fake bonds were sold to the state school fund at prices which alone should have warned the officials. The interest rate was 10 to 12 per cent, and the bonds were offered at a discount of 15 to 20 per cent of the par value. Evidently the state officials were gullible, or perhaps they were friends of the swindlers, as was sometimes suspected and in a few instances proved. The most palpable frauds were committed in Comanche, Harper, Barber, and Ness counties. All of these counties had to be dissolved and reorganized because of the duplicity of the criminals.

In the days when swindlers were abroad in the land, every clump of bunch grass became, in their representation, a human habitation. If there wasn't enough bunch grass, a prairie-dog burrow was listed as "the home of John and Mary ——." These talented promoters gave names to the coyotes and even the jackrabbits that roamed the prairies, their names being selected from directories of eastern cities or from hotel registers in faraway towns. Many honest and worthy citizens of other states would have been considerably shocked to learn that they were listed as residents of a Kansas township, that they had signed petitions requesting the organization of a Kansas county (which had two bona fide residents at the time), that they had voted bonds for schools which were never built and in which it was proposed to instruct children they did not have. Comanche County alone paid out $72,000 in fraudulent bonds to build a courthouse that was never designed and to construct bridges over dry creek beds.

Not only did the swindlers organize the county and proceed to vote the bonds, but they elected one of their own members, a man named Mowry, as a representative and sent him to Topeka to see to it that the state legislature did not investigate too closely the validity of the bonds. Before Mowry was ejected from the legislature he was able to get a bill passed enabling the county to issue $40,000 in bonds. Later he was elected representative from Doniphan County but was thrown out in 1876, arrested, and prosecuted for defrauding the government. He was subsequently released for lack of evidence.

During a special session of the Kansas legislature held in September, 1874, to enact laws for the relief of farmers who had lost their crops in the grasshopper raids, one William H. Horner, representative from Harper County, asked to be seated, asserting that he had received 256 votes in that county. A group of men led by Horner had concocted the scheme and had used names from a Cincinnati, Ohio, directory on a petition for the organization of the county. A. L. Williams, attorney general of Kansas who conducted an investigation into activities in Harper County, wrote:

> The job was conceived in Baxter Springs. A team was hired, a camp outfit and grub for the trip procured and several loafers around the saloons were hired at three dollars a day for the occasion. The saloon bummers were the ones who gave the whole thing away after they came back, being somewhat disgruntled when they discovered that they had been made the catspaws of Horner and the others.[1]

Before Horner was exposed and dismissed from the legislature he and his confederates had each received $10,000 from the scheme.

In Barber County $140,000 in bonds were voted for a courthouse and a railroad. The courthouse was never even designed, and it was said that the railroad "originated in the minds of the boodlers and terminated in their pockets." When the citizens of Barber County discovered what had happened, they rounded up the swindlers (who had elected themselves to county offices) and prepared to hang them from the nearest cottonwood tree. The swindlers, being smooth and seductive liars, persuaded

[1] A. L. Williams, Attorney General's Report, 1876, *Collections* of the Kansas Historical Society, Vol. XII, 206–207.

the irate citizens to free them on the condition that they help undo the evil they had committed. The citizens relented, and the swindlers were allowed to leave. They took the county seal with them to Hutchinson, where they issued more of the fraudulent bonds.

Ness County was organized by Dr. S. G. Rodgers, who brought a small group of people from Chicago and settled them at Smallwood, which was to be the county seat. A petition asking for organization of the county and signed by 600 residents was presented to the governor. The petition was granted, and officers were named. Later it was discovered that there were only twelve actual settlers in the area at the time. Rodgers also got himself elected to the legislature, though not for long. A committee was named to investigate the situation, and when the inhabitants were nowhere to be found, Dr. Rodgers was hastily removed. In the meantime he had sold county and school-district bonds in the east and quickly disappeared when he was accused by the legislature of fraud.

Colonel Sam N. Wood, one of the heroes of the pre-statehood border wars, was charged with complicity in some of these schemes. It was also alleged that he helped issue fraudulent bonds for waterworks and sugar mills in various sections of the state. But he was never prosecuted for these malpractices and was later killed in a county-seat war.

Many counties, legally organized in the boom days, were dissolved when the booms ended. Wallace County, organized in 1868 and dissolved by the state supreme court in 1875, sent a representative to the state legislature in 1887 to get the county reorganized. A special committee headed by T. A. McNeal, member of Barber County, was appointed by the legislature to make an investigation. McNeal, later a famous editor and speaker, revealed his talents as a humorist in the report of the committee:

Within the past two years the tide of emigration has again turned toward Wallace county. The grasshopper no longer sits by the deserted shanty and with his rear limbs plays a doleful accompaniment to the coyote's sad refrain. The newspaper man again lifts up his truthful hymn of praise, and the stranger is beguiled by the land agent's siren song.

Under the impression that they had a valid organization, the citizens of Wallace county have elected county officers, among them a probate judge, whose office is open for medical, scientific and mechanical purposes. He has also issued marriage licenses, and by virtue of his supposed authority various citizens of Wallace county have been married and given in marriage. It seems to be feared by some of the citizens that to fail to recognize the old organization might place a check upon matrimonial felicity.

While we admit that there does not seem to have been any very good reason why the organization of Wallace County should have been declared null and void, and while we fully realize the inconvenience which must arise from this fact, we are nevertheless forced to conclude that the supreme court has so decided, and until that decision is reversed or set aside Wallace County has no legal organization.[2]

Later, however, the county was reorganized.

Garfield County was declared to be illegally organized because of lack of territory. The supreme court decision in this case followed the hotly contested battle between Ravanna and Eminence, one of the worst of the county-seat wars in the state. When the court declared against the county and attached the territory to Finney County, both towns disappeared from the map.

[2] T. A. McNeal (chairman), *Report* of Special Committee Appointed to Investigate the Status of Wallace County (State of Kansas, 1887).

10. *The County-Seat Wars*

O NE OF the lurid periods of Kansas history is marked by the bitter struggles of promoters to win the county seat for their towns. In one such instance, five people were killed, and the Kansas National Guard was called upon seven times to quell riotous actions stimulated by town promoters who were aided and abetted by property owners, businessmen, and hired gangsters.

The county-seat wars began during the territorial days and continued throughout the formation of the state and its divisions. The plum which was sought was the selection of a townsite as the permanent seat of local government, a selection which was tantamount to riches for the promoter and owners of property. The contests were vicious and often bloody. Sometimes they were settled in a single pitched battle; at other times they were settled at the polls. But whether the battle was fought with bullets or ballots, these sessions were played for keeps. It was almost always the rule that the losing town was destined to wither on the vine and ultimately disappear.

In fact, the bitterness of some of the county-seat campaigns remains to this day, for the acrimony engendered has descended unto the second and third generations in the few defeated towns that survived the battle.

Among the more notable of the Kansas county-seat wars were the following:

Topeka *vs.* Tecumseh (Shawnee County)
Ness City *vs.* Sidney (Ness County)
Anthony *vs.* Harper (Harper County)
Atwood *vs.* Blakeman, Herndon, and Ludell (Rawlins County)
Cimarron *vs.* Ingalls (Gray County)

Crawford *vs.* Lyons (Rice County)

Erie *vs.* Chanute (Neosho County)

Goodland *vs.* Itaska, Eustis, and Sherman Center (Sherman County)

Gove *vs* Grainfield (Gove County)

Hugoton *vs.* Woodsdale (Stevens County)

Lakin *vs.* Hartland (Kearny County)

Leoti *vs.* Coronado (Wichita County)

Liberal *vs.* Fargo Springs and Springfield (Seward County)

Lyndon *vs.* Osage City, Superior, and Burlingame (Osage County)

Howard, Boston, and Sedan *vs.* Moline, Peru, and Elk Falls (Howard County) (resulting in the division of Howard County into Elk and Chautauqua counties)

Marysville *vs.* Frankfort, Blue Rapids, and Waterville (Marshall County)

El Dorado *vs.* Augusta, Whitewater, Chelsea, and County Center (Butler County)

Meade *vs.* Carthage (Meade County)

Mound City *vs.* Linnville (Linn County)

Ulysses *vs.* Appomattox (Grant County)

Osborne *vs.* Tilden (now Bloomington), Arlington, and Emley City (Osborne County)

Paola *vs.* Osawatomie (Miami County)

Pratt *vs.* Iuka and Saratoga (Pratt County)

St. John *vs.* Stafford (Stafford County)

Syracuse *vs.* Coolidge and Kendall (Hamilton County)

Sublette *vs.* Santa Fé and Satanta (Haskell County)

Westmoreland *vs.* Louisville, St. George, Mount Union, and Wamego (Pottawatomie County)

Russell Springs *vs.* Oakley (Logan County)

Yates Center *vs.* Neosho Falls, Kalida, and Defiance (Woodson County)

An idea of the bitterness existing in western Kansas may be gained from the records of the Kansas militia. In one instance only an officer or two went to look into the situation. In the others entire companies were called into service for varying periods to aid the local officers in maintaining peace and preventing rioting, killing, and the destruction of property.

The militia never fired a shot in the sharp controversies. However, the mere presence of the armed might of the state government had a salutary effect on the hot-blooded patriots. Fortunately, only a few counties, primarily in the southwestern part of the state, actually engaged in gun battles. It was not uncommon for groups of men to go to an opposing town, haul away the county records, and establish the county offices in their own town, sometimes before there was an election, sometimes while the election was going on. Some of the county-seat wars were settled with a cash exchange. Some were marked by the most scurrilous ballot-box-stuffing activity the state has known. Occasionally it was found that more votes were cast for a single town than there were inhabitants in the entire county.

Undoubtedly the worst of the battles was that in Stevens County. The militia was called in twice, and before the episode ended five men had died by violence. Hugoton had been designated as the county seat when a temporary organization was authorized. While Colonel Wood, an active lawyer with a sharp tongue and a biting sarcasm, was promoting the town of Woodsdale, north of Hugoton, another group was backing the town of Voorhees, south of Hugoton. This occurred in 1886. One of the major disputes followed the jockeying for railroad lines, one through Woodsdale and another through Voorhees. It was thought that this would pinch off Hugoton and eliminate the contender. But the bitterness engendered by this method brought so many threats that the militia was called in to protect the county commissioners, who were canvassing the ballots cast in the railroad-bond elections. At one of the railroad meetings at Voorhees, Colonel Wood was scheduled to make a speech but was unable to attend and sent a copy of his message to James Geraud, who attempted to read it. Geraud was hit over the head by Sam Robinson, town marshal of Hugoton. All attempts to arrest Robinson failed. Some time later he and a group of friends went into No Man's Land, now Beaver County, Oklahoma, to gather plums. A posse of Woodsdale men, headed by Sheriff Cross, started after Robinson and his party. The posse camped with a party of men haying on the prairie. During the evening, the posse was suddenly set upon, lined up, and shot down in cold blood. Sheriff Cross, Theodosius Eaton, Bob Hubbard, and Rolla Wilcox were killed. Herbert Tonney was shot through the shoulder and feigned death until the murderers had left. He then crawled to his horse and returned to tell the story of what has since been known as the Hay Meadow Massacre.

The men participating in the murders were tried at Paris, Texas, convicted, and sentenced to death. However, the judgment was reversed and the case never came to trial a second time. Colonel Wood met a violent death also during the Stevens County dispute. In 1891 he had played a prominent part in the impeachment proceedings against Theodosius Botkin, a biased, partisan protégé of his, then serving as judge of the district court. When the trial resulted in acquittal and Botkin returned to the bench, Colonel Wood, his wife, and a neighbor drove to Hugoton to look after some legal business and attend the court session. As Colonel Wood started to leave the courtroom he was shot and killed by James Brennan, who had been a witness for the defendants in the "hay-meadow" murder trials. Brennan was tried in halfhearted fashion, and when hard times came to Stevens County in the nineties, the county officials refused to spend additional money for extradition of the hay-meadow murderers or for the trials of others active in the bloody affairs of the county. As a result, no one, not even Brennan, was ever punished.

William Easton Hutchison of Garden City was among the last of the active participants in the county-seat wars. He came to Kansas from Pennsylvania, started his law practice at Harper, and then moved to Grant County—right into the midst of the contest between Ulysses, Surprise, and Cincinnati. Later the town of Appomattox was founded about halfway between Surprise and Cincinnati, after which these two towns were invited to move aside and let the county-seat contest be decided between Appomattox and Ulysses, a contest Ulysses was sure to win. Hutchison was county attorney of Grant County at this time. In the election Ulysses won on the face of the returns; however, the Supreme Court threw out so many ballots as fraudulent that another election had to be held. Ulysses won again.

When Judge Botkin resigned after his impeachment, Hutchison was named judge of the district court and served in that capacity for many years. Then he opened a law office at Garden City and later was appointed to the supreme court. He retired at the close of his term in 1938 and returned to private law practice.

There was one death in the Ingalls-Cimarron feud during this period, but it has long been regarded as an accident and not a deliberate murder. The county clerk, a resident of Ingalls, had, with other Ingalls promoters, hired so-called "Hessians" from Dodge City to help move the county records from the county seat, Cimarron, to Ingalls. Quite naturally, the Cimarron residents took up arms and began shooting. An unarmed spectator was killed by a stray bullet—apparently a case of the innocent bystander.

More gunplay comes to light in the Coronado story. In this incident the county-seat contest furnished the background, while the actual battle was only one of many. A group of "tough hombres" from Leoti went over to Coronado to have some fun, so they said. The fun, it developed, was to make Coronado citizens dance to the tune of revolvers popping and bullets ricocheting from the floor. Coronado residents grew tired of the fun after a while and hunted up some guns of their own. A pitched battle followed in which three of the visitors were killed and four Coronado citizens were wounded.

In Seward, Pratt, Haskell, and Gray counties the building of the railroads had much to do with the settlement of the county-seat disputes. Fargo Springs and Springfield both sought the Seward County nomination, but the promoters of each town thought they could win by forcing the Rock Island, then building to the southwest, to route its rails through their town. Although land was offered for a right of way and terminals, bonds were refused. So the Rock Island simply moved its surveying crews, bypassed both towns, and went to Liberal. The defeated towns soon disappeared.

Liquor played a part in one contest. In Pratt County, the towns of Pratt, Iuka, and Saratoga formed a three-cornered contest. A meeting was called at Cullison, a neutral point where the promoters could present the fine advantages of their respective towns. The Iuka promoters never showed up, and later it was charged that some of the Pratt promoters, instead of going to the meeting, had lured the Iuka promoters into a hotel room and filled them so full of liquor they couldn't attend. Pratt got the coveted award.

In the instance where cash figured in the settlement of a county-seat dispute, Marysville is the town that dug up the money. At one time there was evidence that the town was going to lose its designation as the county seat, so the citizens raised $15,000 among themselves, and the town voted $25,000 in bonds for a courthouse and site. Never again would they submit to another election on the county seat question. (Incidentally, Marysville paid off the last of the bonds in 1941.)

The newspapers in the towns battling it out for ascendancy as the county seat offer an able source for the manner in which the wars were waged. The driving purpose of editors operating in rival towns was the annihilation of their neighboring competition and the destruction of its claims. The first person a town promoter sought was an editor. About the only requirements laid down were that the editor be the owner of a shirt-tail full of type and a battered old press and have a command

(*above*) First known photograph of Wichita (1870)
(*below*) North Main Street, Wichita (1871)

of abusive language intended to tear to pieces whatever up-start might undertake to publish a newspaper, alleged or real, in the other community.

The things those editors said about each other were not nice, to put it mildly, but there is reason to believe they meant most of what they wrote, as witness these excerpts:

From the *Hugoton Herald* in the Stevens County war:

Now if we had Sam Wood and the deadheads, who came over from Springfield to attend to our business, tarred and feathered, we would have our dirty work done for the spring. The adherents of Wood are an itinerant class of gamblers, toughs and disreputable roustabouts, the most despicable followers the heart of such a con-temptible old villain could wish.

From the *Cimarron Jacksonian*, in the contest between In-galls and Cimarron, in Gray County:

We are onto the lopeared, lantern-jawed, half-bred and half-born whisky-soaked, pox-eaten pup who pretends to edit that worthless wad of subdued paper known as the Ingalls Messenger. He is just starting out to climb the journalistic banister and wants us to knock the hayseed out of his hair, pull the splinters out of his stern and push him on and up. We'll fool him. No free advertis-ing from us.

By E. L. Cline, editor of the *Eminence Call*, in the Garfield County contest:

The most degraded of bats was one who flourished as editor of a newspaper called the 'Ravanna Record.' He flies from one cor-ner of the rookery which, by the way, was intended for a court-house, to another, regardless of stone walls or contact therewith. His cheek is of flint, and the indentions in some places have almost worn through the walls. He is a great curiosity to every visitor of the deserted village, and oftentimes since have men well versed in veracity tried to win from him his laurels as a liar, but in every in-

61

stance met with disasterous failure. He stands alone more than the peer of any liar on the earth or in the sun, moon, or stars, the balance of the universe still to hear from. For this fame he has become immortal and will continue to eke out a miserable batlike existence until some undiscovered planet will send forth an expert who will rob him of his fame, then, like Samson, shorn of his locks, he will sink into insignificance and pull the dilapidated walls of the rookery down upon him.

The Chieftain, published at Ravanna, referred to the *Garfield County Call* as the *Gall*. In reply the *Call* said:

Poor fool. Go off and soak your head and do not try to defend the $2,500 Boodle Bull any more, for you can't tell lies without losing what little brains you have got and saying just the opposite of what you mean. As for Ravanna—Unhappy Ravanna. She is in the last throes of the death struggle.

The *Call* continued:

Ravanna was a hamlet conceived in infamy and buried in disgrace.

The *Chieftain* replied:

Eminence is thriving like a potatoe bug in an onion patch.

The *Eminence Call* said:

Although in the interest of humanity, common decency, and honest government we desire that this enterprising, God-fearing and progressive city of Ravanna shall be and remain the permanent county seat of this magnificent county, dowered by nature with a climate that makes the most favored part of Italy seem by comparison like a fever-breeding, miasmatic swamp, yet we refuse, in speaking of the denizens of that nondescript collection of bug-infested huts which its few and scabby inhabitants have the supreme gall to call a town, a few miles distant, to descend to the depths of filth and indecency indulged in by the loathsome creature who sets the type for an alleged newspaper in that God-forsaken collection of places unworthy to be called human habitations.

While we can only think of that loathsome tramp with shuddering contempt, our loathing is mingled with a certain degree of pity. He of course was not responsible for the fact that he was born a complete degenerate and fitted out with a face that causes children to scream with fright and old, staid farm horses to break their halters and run away when they see him coming toward them. Those who have known him from childhood say that the first sentence he ever uttered was a lie and since then he has never told the truth except on compulsion.

His first known crime was stealing the pennies from the eyes of his dead grandmother and his next was robbing the cup of a blind organ grinder. He is the kind of a man who sleeps on a manure pile from choice and whose breath has been known to turn the stomach of a veteran skunk.

We only indulge in this description of his person in order to satisfy the curiosity of such of our readers as have never had the misfortune to see him, so that they may be spared being nauseated by getting in his vicinity.

The rival editor replied by saying that he could not waste space on a man who disproved the Darwinian theory; it was impossible that any monkey could have been the ancestor of such a monstrosity and that the only reason this editor "had not been hung long ago was that it was impossible to keep the rope from slipping over his head. In fact he did not have a head, his neck had simply grown up and haired over." "There was a tradition," he continued, "that at one time he did have what seemed to be a head, but that a wen had grown up beside it. He was taken to have the wen removed. The surgeon being somewhat nearsighted and in a hurry, cut off the head and left the wen and the editor's own folks didn't discover the difference for a month afterward."

Neither of these rival towns had more than 400 actual voters, but at the county-seat election one town polled 17,000 votes and the other 18,000. The town casting the smaller number started a contest, the editor asking "whether our boasts about a free ballot and a fair count meant anything, or have the liberties of the people been destroyed by the most unprincipled villains who ever stuffed a ballot box?"

The *Ravanna Chieftain* said:

We too might have resorted to fraud, but our citizens, relying on their constitutional rights and believing that there could not be such shameless villainy in this free land, decided to allow only legal votes to be counted; but the human hyenas shall not prevail. If the courts are too cowardly or too venal to rebuke such outrages then a brave God-fearing people will rise up in their wrath and smite these polluted lepers hip and thigh.

The debate grew progressively worse, and when the charge of fraudulent voting came before the supreme court, the judges held that the county did not come up to the constitutional requirements about area and ordered the county dissolved. As previously mentioned, Garfield County became Garfield Township of Finney County.

Even in later years county-seat elections were called because a rival town sought to have the county seat moved. Russell Springs, Winona, and Oakley, all in Logan County, had contests over the location of the county seat long after it had been determined. Location, of the towns, railroad connections, and other considerations have generally caused the renewal of the disputes. Gove and Grainfield have staged recent campaigns for the county seat of Gove County.

But the most active recent county-seat contest was in Morton County, when Elkhart sought to have the county seat removed from Richfield. To date the voters have said "no" in every election. Once before, Elkhart and Richfield tangled on the county-seat question, when Richfield won by 26 votes.

Elkhart is 27 miles from Richfield and is situated in the southwestern corner of the county, while Richfield is almost in the exact center. By reason of its convenient location Richfield won, but that town has a population of between 50 and 70, while Elkhart has nearly one thousand, or about one-half the population of the county. The burning of the courthouse at Richfield on January 22, 1950, may be expected to produce a third contest for the county seat.

11: *Skulduggery—Yes, We Had Some Once*

KANSAS has brought forth many unusual projects, but few are more outstanding than the Committee on Skulduggery established by the Wyandotte Constitutional Convention in July, 1859. State and national committees named to investigate nefarious activities are no rarity, but so far as can be determined the Kansas Committee on Skulduggery is the only such committee ever given so descriptive a title.

The late Ben F. Simpson, member of the committee and later attorney general of Kansas, tells his impressions of the work of the committee, which mainly concerned itself with the activities surrounding the selection of the state capital:

I could never fathom what it was in the history of Kansas that has caused a cruel fate to decree, at the close of every deliberative body held in the state there should be a disgraceful supplement in the shape of an investigating committee. The constitutional convention was no exception to the operation of this rule—abounding in shame, and giving birth, sustenance and employment to an infinite number of the flannel-mouthed whelps of that foul hag, Mrs. Candor, whose mendacious tongues and contentious lips caused more well-defined and specific stenches to arise than could possibly be manufactured in the city of Cologne. This particular disgrace was occasioned by the statement of a delegate from Doniphan county, E. M. Hubbard, that Wm. Hutchinson, one of the delegates from Douglas county, had offered him a good lot if he would vote for Lawrence as the temporary capital of the state. On this statement becoming known to the members of the convention, an investigating committee was ordered, appointed and commenced its labors.

Hubbard swore to the truth of his statement; Hutchinson denied under oath. Hubbard then swore that the delegate from Douglas was a liar, and the delegate from Douglas, being duly sworn, deposed that the delegate from Doniphan was "another." And thus ended the testimony. The committee reported the facts to the convention, and the whole subject was laid upon the table —the usual parliamentary resort when no one knew what else to do.[1]

It may be gathered from this report that there was great rivalry among the various towns over the selection of a temporary state capital. Later, when the first legislature ordered a vote on the question of the permanent capital, there were votes for some 50 towns.

The Committee on Skulduggery reported to the convention the evidence it secured. This report was laid on the table, and since nothing was ever done about it, the secretary of the convention did not enter the details of the investigation in the convention records. It may be, of course, that there actually wasn't any skulduggery going on in the convention, as the report of the committee and subsequent actions of the convention would seem to indicate. But it is also possible that the committee did not choose to investigate matters too closely.

C. K. Holliday, founder of Topeka and of the Atchison, Topeka, and Santa Fé Railway System, spent a good deal of time at Wyandotte during the convention and wrote regularly

[1] From "Reprint of Proceedings on Debate, Wyandotte Constitutional Convention" (State of Kansas, 1920).

to his wife back in Meadville, Pennsylvania. In a letter[2] dated July 14 he wrote:

Today the chances are altogether in our favor and I now think we will get the capital located at our place. But the trickery of politicians may change this expectation. I have said or done little for myself while here. I have no doubt my advocacy of the capital matter will materially injure my political prospects, but if the convention will locate the capital for five years at Topeka (what we ask) I am willing to be defeated for a year or two to come.

Evidently Holliday wielded considerable influence in the convention, for on July 24 he wrote his wife:

I dropped you a line yesterday informing you of the important fact that the convention has located the capital at Topeka. This is certainly a great triumph—and will greatly enhance the prospects of our town and of our property.

It kills me politically, however, for a time at least—but present pecuniary good is worth more to me than prospective political position.

Holliday gave up whatever ambitions he had to be governor or United States senator, though he was mentioned for both offices several times. His reference to the trickery of politicians and his statement, quoted above, about "pecuniary good" certainly indicates that he made some promises in order to win the capital for Topeka.

[2] Quoted in *Kansas Historical Quarterly*, Vol. VI (1937).

1 2: *Illiteracy on the Run*

M
ANY OUTLANDERS often ask how it is that Kansas
stands so high in literacy records compiled by the
government and other statistical bureaus. The
newspapers are willing to take most of the credit
for this, and they cite the fact that throughout its history the
Sunflower State has had more newspapers than any other state,
including such populous ones as New York and Pennsylvania.
Moreover, the state stands high in the number of youths attending high schools and colleges.

It has surprised many people, including some Kansans, to
learn that the state stands at the top in number of newspapers.
The *Union List of Newspapers,* published by the Bibliographi-
cal Society of America in 1937,[1] issued the results of its survey of newspapers in the United States from 1821 to 1936.
According to this list, 4,368 newspapers were published in
Kansas during the 115 years covered by the compilation. New
York was second with 3,309 and Pennsylvania third with
2,519. Kansas was also shown to have more library entries for
newspapers than the Library of Congress: the library of the
Kansas State Historical Society has 4,813 separate listings,
while the Library of Congress has 4,588.

The collection of newspapers in the Historical Society has
long stood at the top in this country. The society has 52,836
bound volumes of newspapers published in Kansas and 10,000
bound volumes of newspapers published outside the state since
1767.

In 1950 there were 697 newspapers and periodicals published in Kansas: 58 were published daily, 12 were published
semiweekly, 2 triweekly, 383 weekly, 18 fortnightly, 25 semi-

[1] H. W. Wilson Company.

monthly, 2 were published every three weeks, 129 monthly, 16 bimonthly, 28 quarterly, 2 semiannually, 2 annually, 3 once each six weeks, and 17 were published occasionally.

Kansas began to foster newspapers in the very early days. Jotham Meeker published the first periodical in Kansas in 1835. The publication, the *Shawnee Sun*, was not a newspaper in the present sense of the word, but a monthly paper devoted chiefly to the religious work of the Baptist missionaries among the Shawnee Indians and to the affairs of the Delawares and Potawatomis. Since these tribes had no written language, Meeker arbitrarily assigned English letters to the Indian sounds. Donald C. McMurtrie, who has made an exhaustive study of Meeker's work, points out that in the publications for the Shawnees the English letter *b* represented the sound *th*, as in "thin," while for the Delawares the same letter represented the sound *u*, as in "tube."[2]

The first regular newspaper was the *Kansas Weekly Herald*, which began publication at Leavenworth on September 15, 1854. William H. Adams set up the type for the first issue under an elm tree, and the records disclose that the newspaper actually antedated the town in which it was published. A description of the town at that time reads:

Four tents, all on one street, a barrel of water or whiskey under a tree, and a pot on a pole over the fire. Under a tree a type-sticker had his case before him and was at work on the first number of the new paper, and within a frame, without a board on side or roof, was the editor's desk and sanctum.

This was the beginning of the newspaper activity which was destined to become an important part of Kansas life. In the early days of the state a printer could often be found among the promoters of a town. He might be the first settler on a new townsite and publish a newspaper full of glowing accounts of

[2] *Kansas Historical Quarterly*, Vol. I (1831–32).

the town and its prospects, long before a single building had been erected. Some of the newspapers listed in the files of the Historical Society are actually nothing more than boom editions issued solely to persuade people to invest in lots in a new town.

The oldest paper in Kansas, so far as continuous publication is concerned, is the *Leavenworth Times*, established in March, 1857. Next comes the *Kansas Chief*, established by Sol Miller at White Cloud on June 4, 1857. In July, 1872, Miller moved his paper to Troy and published the first issue of *The Chief* in that city on July 4. The *Oskaloosa Independent* is the only paper in Kansas published for 90 years by the same family. The newspaper was established on July 11, 1860, and John Roberts, the present editor, is the third generation of his family associated with it.

Kansas newspapers have always taken a very active part in the affairs of the communities in which they are published. The editors of the early days were men of strong opinions, and since their papers were personal organs, they expressed their views in no uncertain terms. There was much violence attendant on the publication of early-day newspapers. The first one to be wrecked was the *Territorial Register* at Leavenworth. Missourians who did not like the political views of the editor on the slavery question crossed the ice-covered Missouri River on December 22, 1855, tossed the type into the street, and dumped the press into the river through a hole in the ice. The following spring and summer the *Free State* and the *Herald of Freedom*, both published at Lawrence, were destroyed by a proslavery crowd who raided the town.

During the Populist days and the years following, the number of papers in the state increased tremendously. There were Republican, Democratic, and Populist papers, and a few of other political beliefs. In every community every organization having anything to do with political affairs had an organ of its own. The result was that in many of the county seats there would be four to six weekly newspapers, each of a different political faith. At the turn of the century many of these papers became dailies, and it was not uncommon for a Kansas city of three or four thousand inhabitants to have two or more daily newspapers, each with a tabloid wire service for world news, but devoted primarily to local news and political affairs. Few of the papers that were founded purely as political organs were able to stand alone after the close of the political campaigns which brought them into being. As a result, many weekly papers throughout the state have consolidated, and only a few cities in the state now support more than one daily. Many of the county seats which formerly supported one or two dailies now have none at all.

At the close of the Civil War there were 37 regular newspapers in Kansas (the same number existing in the Thirteen Colonies at the time the Declaration of Independence was written). The number grew apace as the state was settled and boomed in the last three decades of the nineteenth century. Early in the twentieth century the number of papers declined as people began to demand quality in place of quantity in their newspapers and the ravings and rantings of the rugged individualists among editors ceased to be of interest to their readers.

1 3: *When Editorial Frankensteins Were in Style*

THE VOICE of the Kansas editor has carried far—yea, even to Washington, New York, San Francisco, the way stations between, to London, and to Paris. For the Kansas editor has always been forthright and vigorous, the product of a land which was born in politics and grew up in times of turbulence and violence. His primary purpose was to fit the new state into his conception of an ideal commonwealth.

When Kansas was young, everybody was in politics, more or less. When it was a territory, there were a dozen elections within two years in which slavery was the sole question at issue. The result was extremely partisan and bitter campaigning on both sides.

The Kansas editor never shunned his responsibilities. He did not believe in being neutral and took sides on every question. "The spirit of the people was adventurous, self-centered, impatient of slow progress and indifferent to the danger of trying experiments," wrote Captain Henry King, editor and one of the founders of the *Kansas Magazine*. "It was in our politics, perhaps, that we were most apt to disregard the impulses of brotherly kindness and patience. The Kansas newspapers had early manifested a partiality for aggressive and vociferous campaigning ... The Kansas Press has ever been noted for its high standard of excellence. You will search its files in vain for vibrations of unintelligence, for specimens of puerile or slovenly workmanship. There can be no 'aspersions on its parts of speech'; there are no orphaned verbs or widowed nouns ludicrously splotching its record."[1]

[1] *Kansas Magazine*, Vol. I (1872).

Jim Lane, firebrand leader of the abolitionist forces in the early days and one of the first United States senators from Kansas, often remarked about the lambastings administered to him by the *Atchison Champion* when John J. Ingalls, later also a United States senator, was editor. "The mildest term it ever applied to me was miscreant," Lane said.

In the days before the turn of the present century nearly every editor had a pseudonym, which he usually referred to as a Frankenstein. Mrs. Percy B. Shelley created Frankenstein as the protagonist of a novel who later destroyed his creator, but nothing like that happened to the Kansas Frankensteins. They were useful and important adjuncts of many newspaper offices and helpful friends of the editor. Even into the present century the Frankenstein was in full flower, though he gradually dropped out of the ken of most newspaper readers with the death of the editor who created him. Editors of the second and third generation did not take time to think up a suitable name for a Frankenstein of their own. The most important Frankenstein still in operation and going strong is Ima Washout, the pal of Miss Bertha Shore of the *Augusta Gazette*. Ima was born when an advertiser folded and Miss Shore was assigned the job of filling the space with lively chitchat. "I have often been sorry that I spawned Ima," said Miss Shore. "She has embarrassed me many times. She isn't an old maid because she was married once for about three weeks and found that the man who promised to lay the world at her feet meant the family wash and three relatives. She is large, boisterous and hates malicious gossip. She likes kids and has expressed the idea that kids get along pretty well in spite of their parents. She wears a petticoat and is often found with a high octane concoction, two parts gin, one part brandy and one part Lydia Pinkham. She has tried to learn to smoke a cob pipe and to roll her own cigarettes and has failed in both."

It has often been said that the editorial Frankenstein is strictly a product of Kansas, since few editors outside the Sunflower State have resorted to this mode of editorial expression. It has been a successful means of diverting suspicion from the true creators of pungent notes about Kansas politics and politicians. It was once declared that "the Kansas Frankenstein is the interpreter of the grass roots. It is the direct primary of Kansas thought. It is the voice of the people." For many years Kansans looked carefully every week in the better-known newspapers for the bits of philosophy and wit they felt sure would appear. Little did Kansans know how eagerly the editors of the eastern press copied and gloried in the expressive comments of the Kansas brethren. It was often pointed out by eastern editors that Kansans took the products of the Frankensteins as a matter of course, while those outside the state looked upon their yield as an important contribution to journalism. A lean year among the Frankensteins was well-nigh a calamity.

Drake Watson and the Hon. Abner Handy were the two best known Frankensteins in Kansas. E. W. Howe, editor of the Atchison Globe, was the creator of Drake Watson, while William Allen White of the *Emporia Gazette* aided and abetted the political views of the Hon. Handy, who was often pointed out as the most terrible example of reactionism. Drake Watson and Ab Handy generally held a viewpoint opposite to that of their pseudonym. Drake Watson made biting comments about politics and the foibles of women in general. Parson Twine, an aged Negro preacher at Atchison, was frequently quoted by Howe, but most of the sayings credited to Parson Twine were actually Howe's. The Hon. Abner Handy was a political hack who worked with the reactionary elements within the Republican party and was "agin" every progressive move. He was rewarded with small jobs in the legislature and served as messenger and doorkeeper in county and state conventions and finally landed a postmastership. His slogan was "Ab Handy never sleeps," when it came to loyalty to his political friends.

Ole Bill Shiftless was the philosopher of the late B. P. Walker, editor of the *Osborne Farmer*. Ole Bill and work never got along, and they managed to dodge each other fairly well until the dry-goods stores began to receive merchandise in cardboard boxes, and Ole Bill could no longer sit on wooden packing cases and whittle while his cronies gathered around to discuss current news and politics.

The Village Deacon was another of Walker's philosophical Frankensteins. The Deacon was suave and sophisticated but lacked the incisive force of Ole Bill.

Miss Maybelle Gaddy was the Frankenstein of Charles M. Vernon of the *Manhattan Mercury*. Miss Gaddy was a young lady of some twenty summers who was to be seen regularly on Main Street and who never neglected an opportunity to walk past the pool halls or other places where the lads were likely to be loafing. Though she walked along haughtily with her chin in the air, she considered the days successful when a boy walked home with her.

Charles A. Blakesley of *The Kansas City Star* invented three Frankensteins for his "Kansas Notes" who brought him a considerable amount of fame. His creations were Professor Clinker, who worked at the Cinderbeetle quarantine station at Coolidge (a sinecure political job); Judge Adna P. Gristlebone, chief inspector for the cinderbeetles; and Major Franklin Osgood, who was the chief tormenter and enemy of Judge Gristlebone. The judge always asserted that when the cinderbeetles invaded Kansas and began devouring the rails, bridges, and wire fences, he gave up his law practice and his real estate and loan office to join in the crusade against the pests, which caused Major Osgood to remark that he didn't believe the judge ever had any law practice and that the judge had always been a political leech who wouldn't live long if he didn't have a political job. The two old codgers were always snorting at each other and produced many lively comments about men and affairs in the Sunflower State.

J. L. Brady of the *Lawrence Journal* created Bill Sincaller of Vineland and through him commented on the hair styles and other aspects of the women of the community. Clyde Knox of the *Sedan Times-Star* brought into being Professor Silas Pewter, the sage of the Flint Hills who farmed by day according to accepted theories and wrote columns for the paper by night on his own peculiar notions about farming.

Squire Thrifty, who appeared for J. L. Napier in the *Newton Journal*, tried to live up to his name by deploring the ways of the people of the community who spent all their money on what he termed riotous living. Nutty Ned was the poetical pseudonym of Imri Zumwalt of the *Bonner Springs Chieftain*. He was regarded as a wise old owl because he did not usually indulge in the airy persiflage of the ordinary citizen.

Judge Pettingill was the alias under which Herbert Cavaness embellished the *Chanute Tribune* with such whole-souled philosophy as

We would find more good in our neighbors if we would quit wearing goggles when looking for virtues and searching for faults with a microscope.

Adam Croaker was the Frankenstein of M. M. Beck of the *Holton Recorder*. He really was the antithesis of his name, for Adam was anything but an old croaker, and his creator revealed a quaint philosophy behind the inappropriate name.

Homer Hoch, son of a former governor, long a member of Congress, and later an associate justice of the Kansas supreme court, edited his father's newspaper, the *Marion Record*, when his father was working the Chautauqua circuit. Cy Knocker was his Frankenstein, a man who insisted that every public improvement in the town would be made over his prostrate form, and generally was. Bill Booster, another Hoch creation, was eternally boosting the town and its people and devoting more time to civic affairs than to his own business. But he got things done.

A. F. Riddle succeeded his father as the editor of the Minne-

Cyrus K. Holliday
Founder of Topeka and first president of the
Atchison, Topeka and Santa Fe Railroad

apolis, Kansas, *Messenger*. Father and son had often talked about the need for a philosopher with horse sense. Peter Doubt, the creation of the younger man, filled that need. "There were times when we did not feel like treading on thin ice on some project," said Mr. Riddle. Then Doubt would write a letter to the editor and present views about the projects which were often directly opposite to the opinions of the editors. In this way the interest of the community would be aroused.

Tom Thompson of the *Howard Courant* had Polk Daniels to aid him in providing homely wit and needed advice to his newspaper clientele. Polk felt that a good many people talked too much, so he limited his observations and discovered that his readers enjoyed the results.

Aunt Jerusalem Grimm, the female moonshiner of Quad-hole Township, was a Frankenstein of Jay Iden, editor of the *Pink Rag* of Topeka. Her mule would take Aunt Jerusalem into the Arkansas hills where the "revenooers" couldn't follow. Iden also created Little Cerise, a boy whose brain had ceased developing when he was eight years old but whose sharp comments about men and affairs caused anger and dismay among his elders.

Austin Butcher of the *Altoona Tribune* had two pseudonyms, Mace Liverwurst and Kate Bender. Mace was the most cheerful liar who ever lived in Kansas, and his braggart yarns about his deeds during the Spanish-American War were the most outlandish tales imaginable. Kate Bender, murderess, served as a commentator on women's affairs.

There were many other Frankensteins in the Kansas newspaper world during the latter half of the nineteenth century and the early years of the twentieth. The readers generally recognized the editor hiding behind the pseudonym, but they enjoyed the sayings just as well. Moreover, they knew where to lay the blame if things went wrong. This method enabled the editor to present to his readers the other side of a question when he was helplessly bound by group loyalties to support some project which he did not believe in. Today the Frankensteins have almost entirely disappeared from Kansas newspapers—an important indication of the modern trend of news presentation and editorial comment.

In the half-century since the heyday of the Frankensteins, the newspapers of America have, in fact, succumbed almost completely to the so-called objective method, at its best, decently informative but never distinguished; at its worst, a poor substitute for the interpretation which the modern age needs. The age of personal journalism in which the Frankensteins of Kansas flourished was an age which demanded and applauded opinion. It is perhaps not overreaching the case to say that the health and liveliness of Kansas journalism today is owing in part, at least, to the survival of the spirit if not the technique of another day. Henry J. Allen, Victor Murdock, Ed Howe, and William Allen White, great men in a long line of journalistic greatness, didn't merely happen. But it is probable that they could have happened only in Kansas. It may properly be said that the last of the rugged individualists, editorially speaking, was the late William Allen White. He conformed to no pattern of politics. He believed in the dignity of man and the right of the individual to do as he pleased, as long as he did not interfere with the rights of others or trespass upon good taste. He used unique language and sometimes expressed opinions in most unorthodox fashion. But those qualities made William Allen White a forceful character who was the despair of the politician and the joy of the citizen.

Although White was a late-comer to the coterie of rugged individualists who raised Kansas newspapers to an exceptionally high plane, he left his mark upon the politics of the state no less effectively than Dan Anthony, M. M. Beck, J. W. Roberts, Noble Prentis, John Speer, Henry King, Sol Miller, Marsh Murdock, Jacob Stotler, Bent Murdock, and lesser lights in the galaxy of editorial stars in the Kansas firmament.

14: *Editors, the Fighting Kind*

IN THE DAYS when the typewriter was yet unknown, Kansas editors carried a pad of paper and a pencil, and many of them also packed pistols, which they were not afraid to use to maintain their dignity and their views. However, they were not actually bloodthirsty. There were only one or two instances of the lust to kill in the rowdy, vituperative, flamboyant, pitiless, and partisan period of Kansas journalism.

In addition to the local editors there was another group of equally vigorous writers—the correspondents for the eastern newspapers, who also toted guns as a part of their journalistic equipment. Like their local colleagues, they used a vigorous language. In this group should be included William A. Phillips, later a member of Congress, for whom Camp Phillips was named in World War II. Others were Horace Greeley, Marcus J. Parrot, Martin F. Conway, Colonel Richard J. Hinton, John Henry Kagi, James Redpath, John E. Cook, Samuel F. Tappen, Richard Realf, and James M. Winchell. Winchell was later named chairman of the Wyandotte Constitutional Convention.

Dan Anthony of Leavenworth stands at the top of the list of fighting editors. He fought a duel, was shot at many times, and on one occasion was seriously wounded. For many years he carried two guns, and even after the need to carry them had lessened, he kept them in the top drawer of his desk in the *Leavenworth Times* office. Once, when a group of men had decided that the paper should not print the facts about a particular incident, Anthony armed an editor with one gun and took the other himself. The two men stood on the top step of the entryway into the *Times* office as the mob came marching along the street. Someone advised the mob's leaders that Anthony was ready for them. There was a short consultation, after which the crowd melted away.

R. C. Satterlee, editor of the *Leavenworth Herald*, was Anthony's first victim. The *Times* editor had heard that a rebel flag was flying in a store at Iatan, Missouri, across the river from Leavenworth. Anthony went over to check on the report, and his own paper soon announced that he had brought the flag back to Leavenworth. The *Herald* copied the *Times* announcement and below it printed another version asserting that Anthony had failed to get the flag. This version concluded, "Thereupon, it is said, Anthony made double quick time out of the state, down the railroad track, with coat tails extended and the utmost horror depicted upon his countenance."

The next day Anthony went gunning for Satterlee. The rival editor was not in his office, but Anthony met him a short distance away, and after a few words the shooting began, resulting in Satterlee's death and the wounding of a friend who had accompanied Anthony.

Near the close of the Civil War Anthony engaged in a violent dispute with Colonel C. R. Jennison. Anthony was supporting Captain J. B. Swain, who was under court-martial at Fort Leavenworth for "killing rebels." Anthony wrote:

Colonel Jennison gave the orders for the killing and when called upon to testify denied his verbal order,

to which Jennison replied in a paid advertisement:

D. R. Anthony, in his statement of May 11th, in regard to me, lied and knew he lied when making it.

Some time later Jennison and Anthony met on the street. They exchanged some shots, and Jennison was severely wounded. Anthony was acquitted of the charge of assault with intent to kill.

W. W. Embry, another rival editor, shot Anthony as he was entering a theater lobby. Later Embry was killed by Thomas Thurston, a former employee of Anthony's. Colonel Anthony was so severely wounded that for some time doctors held no hope for his recovery. That he did survive and lived some forty years after the episode testifies to the endurance of the journalistic species Anthony represented.

Anthony was attacked three times during his first week of residence in Kansas. Since Leavenworth was near the Missouri line and was largely sympathetic to the slave owners, the citizens of Leavenworth determined to rid themselves of this powerful abolitionist. But their determination failed them, and Anthony went on supporting the abolition cause, fighting with fists, guns, and editorial brickbats. After he became mayor of Leavenworth, he quarreled bitterly with General Thomas Ewing about groups of Missourians who were coming into Kansas to claim horses they said had been stolen. One day Anthony was arrested by soldiers, and martial law was declared in Leavenworth. After he was released, his lead editorial stated:

Yesterday I was brutally arrested and marched out of town with two thieves at my side, followed by soldiers with cocked revolvers pointed at my back. Tonight I return to Leavenworth, my home, escorted by a committee of your best and most loyal citizens. Yesterday martial law reigned in Leavenworth, today it is scattered to the four winds of heaven. Yesterday we were despondent, today we are triumphant. The thieves who had me in arrest left in a hurry. Had General Ewing made the same haste when he left here in pursuit of Quantrill, with his enemy in front, that his detectives and soldiers made on an imaginary foe in the rear, Quantrill would not have escaped from the butchery at Lawrence with impunity.

Anthony was never averse to engaging in controversies with anyone. A. F. Collamore, Leavenworth correspondent for the *Kansas City Times*, wrote of him:

The fiendish, bloodthirsty proprietor of the Leavenworth Times is so fearfully low down and utterly despicable where he is thoroughly known, that the very dogs, the sorriest mongrels or the mangiest Spitz, would, in a certain contingency, pass him by, and cross a county writhing in agony in search of a cleaner post. For 22 years it has been his habit to call decent men, who opposed his lunacies, dirty dogs, gamblers, skunks, drunkards, scoundrels, etc. His beastiality of disposition, and brutishness of heart, have banished him from the walk of life of every gentleman and he stalks through our streets, despised, shunned, and hideous in the sight of those who, with gentle instincts or cultivated habits, loathe disagreeable or disgusting surroundings.

Ignoring decency, to answer an argument or refute a charge, he even resorts to his vocabulary of billingsgate which springs spontaneous from a putrid heart, and scatters his blackguardism in very poor English. Gentlemen, congregated on the sidewalk, scatter at his approach, as though a cyclone of epidemic pestilence was imminent, and ladies shudder as they drop their veils and shrink with horror, when they realize his vicinage.

Anthony replied that Collamore and two of his colleagues had "for years been associates and participants in whiskey drinking, gambling and debauchery. The trio embraces three of the lowest, dirtiest, filthiest scoundrels that ever infested any place on earth."

Anthony helped to unseat his own cousin from the governorship. Although he had assisted in the election of George T. Anthony as governor, the two began to disagree on policy early in the term, and when his cousin ran for renomination, Anthony lead the victorious fight against him.

On other battle fronts J. Clarke Swayze, editor of the Topeka Blade, had engaged in sharp editorial controversies with F. P. Baker, editor of the Topeka Commonwealth, and with J. W. Wilson and V. P. Wilson, editors of the Topeka Times. Swayze accused the Wilsons of padding bills for county printing and cast other aspersions on the integrity of his rivals. The Wilsons retaliated and, among other charges, referred to Swayze as a wife beater and child murderer. Wilson later shot and killed Swayze as he emerged from his editorial offices.

For many years J. W. Roberts, founder of the *Oskaloosa Independent*, exposed and condemned the nefarious activities of various residents of Oskaloosa. During one such campaign armed citizens stood guard in the newspaper office all night to thwart an expected attack. For his part, Roberts spent the night at home with three guns by his side. A crude bomb was placed in the doorway of the newspaper office, but it was discovered in time to prevent damage.

After the white-hot anger engendered by the Civil War had cooled, the tossing of bullets between rival editors gradually ceased, to be replaced by satirical invective and verbal abuse.

The late Sol Miller, editor of the *Troy Chief*, was constantly engaged in some sort of controversy with his neighboring editors. Occasionally he went farther afield. The editors of the *Lawrence Republican* once took him to task for the vulgarity of his abuse. Miller replied, "If the road to refinement lies through the channel established by the editors of the Republican we pray that we may remain vulgar."

Of a near-by editor Miller noted:

We have heard of hybrids of various descriptions, but only once of a cross between a quadruped and an insect. That isolated case is the editor of the Iowa Point Dispatch—he is half fyste and half tumble bug. His quadruped nature is indicated by his bark, and his insect nature by the substance he delights to revel in.

The *Marysville Enterprise* and the *Nemaha Courier*, newspapers in adjoining counties, engaged in extensive bickering, and it appears that the editor of the *Courier*, a man named Cone, had insinuated that the Marysville editor had been jailed in a military guardhouse at one time. The *Enterprise* replied:

83

Cone, for the three hundred fifty-fifth time, refers to our being in the guardhouse on one occasion. We have acknowledged that fact so often that it is useless to do so any more. Cone—you idiot, you jackass, redheaded, frizzle-headed, mush-headed, slab-sided, brainless deformity and counterfit imitation of a diseased polecat —we inform you again, once more and emphatically, we were there; but it wasn't for stealing type.

The *Ottawa Republican* and the *Ottawa Journal* sometimes had difficulty getting along, too. The *Republican* wrote about the rival sheet:

For the most fulsome and able-bodied lying we recommend the Ottawa Journal as being in advance of any sheet in Kansas. Their elementary principles are founded upon falsehood and their political contest upon exaggeration of the most exaggerated sort. It has grown to an impossibility for them to make the most common statement about the most common affairs without falsifying and enlarging.

There was great rivalry between Leavenworth and Atchison. Both cities claimed to be the chief commercial metropolis on the Missouri River. H. Rives Pollard, the editor of the *Leavenworth Herald* wrote:

It is with great reluctance we condescend to notice anything from the vituperative pen of the insignificant, puerile, silly blackguard who at present presides over the editorial conduct of the Sovereign. Atchison may be, but Leavenworth is not, the place where Peter Pindar's remark, that "every blackguard scoundrel is a king," is recognized by the community. . . . The egotistical dupe of the Sovereign thinks we are a representative of the verdancy of Virginia. Be that as it may, we can retort by saying that the mendacity of Missouri is represented in the person of R. S. Kelley of Atchison.

84

R. S. Kelley, editor of the *Atchison Squatter Sovereign*, replied that Pollard was the scum of the earth, a blackguard, and a muckraker. Pollard replied:

> The low, silly, garrulous numbskull of the Squatter Sovereign, yclept Kelley, the contemptible, whining, blind puppy of Atchison, that answers to the name of "Bob," continues to pour forth his tirade of abuse upon us with unrelenting fury. . . . The Sovereign, in speaking of our "low-flung language," says, "He assail no one but in the language of the doggery," suitable to the occasion.

The epithets finally roused Pollard to issue a challenge to Kelley. But Kelley replied that if the Leavenworth editor would devote more time to printing the news and helping his community he wouldn't have time to fight a duel.

The fighting editors of Kansas did not spare the lash of harsh words when political leaders, in particular, wandered slightly from the straight and narrow path. And the political leaders lashed back. On one occasion a Kansas governor who had been severely criticized by the newspapers opened a convention speech with the salutation, "Mr. Chairman, ladies, gentlemen, and polecats of the press."

Another Kansas governor sat by a window in the statehouse one day watching a newspaper reporter walk across the grounds. "If someone will shoot that s.o.b., I'll meet him at the door of the prison with a pardon," exclaimed the governor to his visitors and staff.

The late Tom McNeal, a Kansas editor for many years, was inducted into the newspaper business by a bucket of sorghum molasses. His brother had migrated to southwestern Kansas and had urged Tom to move to Barber County. McNeal, who had studied law and had been admitted to the bar, planned to open a law office there. Instead, he became an editor, legislator, speaker, and writer of tall tales and fables. The *Barber County Mail* was then edited by a man named Cochran, a careless printer with little command of language and even less morals. What happened to him is told by McNeal:

> On a decidedly cool night the regulators took the editor from his humble office, stripped him of his clothing and then administered a punishment which I think was entirely unique and unprecedented in the treatment of editors. There was no tar in town and not a feather bed to be opened, but an enterprising settler had brought in a sorghum molasses mill the year before and as sorghum generally grew there, had manufactured a crop into thick, ropy molasses. Owing to the cold weather the molasses was thicker and ropier than usual. The regulators secured a gallon of this, mixed it well with sandburs, and administered this mixture liberally to the nude person of the editor.
>
> I need not tell my readers who are familiar with the nature of the sandbur, that it is an unpleasant vegetable to have attached to one's person. . . .
>
> Other citizens . . . told the editor he could remain as long as he wished and they would be responsible for his safety. Cochran expressed his appreciation [but] confessed to them that the atmosphere of the town did not seem salubrious or congenial to him.

McNeal then became editor of the paper.

Sometimes those offended by the editors resorted to various means of presenting their side of the story to the public. Richard Realf, one of the eastern correspondents, irritated by the jibes of a Lawrence newspaper, replied in a handbill which read:

Notice! !

To the Public!
I, the undersigned, on my own personal honor and responsibility, do hereby publicly declare G. W. Brown, editor of the Herald of Freedom, to be a wilful LIAR, a malicious SLANDERER, and a most contemptible COWARD; all of which charges I hold myself in readiness to prove.

RICHARD REALF

Lawrence, July 14, 1857.

The handbill was printed in the largest type the printer had and was circulated throughout Lawrence by small boys.

There hasn't been a good newspaper row in Kansas for forty years. The late William Allen White practically closed the book on the fighting editors when he wrote:

There is in progress in a small Kansas town, at the present time, a newspaper row that reminds one of the halcyon days when the rag across the street was edited by a lop-eared leper. Unfortunately for the picturesque in journalism, the lop-eared lepers are nearly all dead, or in the poorhouse. We seldom hear of them any more, and we sigh for the touch of a vanished hand, and the sound of a voice that is still.

In this Kansas row, one of the editors is described as a hyena that prowls by night. The hyena that prowls by night replies that his antagonist is, to all intents and purposes, a polecat. The polecat appears slightly dazed by this rebuke, but rallies bravely, and intimates that the hyena would consider it no crime to steal the coppers from the dead man's eyes, although such charges involves nature faking, for what would a hyena do with coppers—or, for that matter, why should a dead man wear them on his eyes?

The hyena ignores this accusation and expresses his profound conviction that the polecat would rob a widow's hen roost. And so the cheerful controversy proceeds. It is really refreshing, as viewed from a distance, and it is too bad that the prominent business men are always butting in to stop it. They ought to be sending marked copies of the local papers all over the country to cheer up a doleful world.[1]

[1] *Emporia Gazette*, November 6, 1907.

15: *When Newspaper Names Made News*

THE QUESTION has been asked, "What's in a name?" Insofar as Kansas newspapers are concerned, the answer is "Almost everything." The names chosen by editors for their newspapers during the early days were, like other cultural manifestations, clearly in keeping with the Age of Freedom. They harmonized with the contemporary dugouts and sod houses of the Kansas prairie in the last third of the nineteenth century.

At this point, however, the analogy must stop, for in all truth many of the newspapers bearing startling names didn't live up to the understandable expectations of their subscribers. The *Scalping Knife*, a newspaper at Cottonwood Falls, was momentarily expected to scalp politicians. But it never did. The *Astonisher and Paralyzer* at Carbondale could certainly be expected to astonish someone at some time or other, and it might even paralyze the hopes of some political shyster or demagogue. But during the two years the paper was published, it gradually became apparent that the editor had put everything into the name.

The *Champion Liar* got under way at Perry, but when the paper didn't live up to its name the disappointed readers soon stopped supplying the long green necessary to keep it going. The *Kansas Korn Knife* and the *Agitator* were published at Garnett. *GunnPowder* was published at Pittsburg, while the *Howitzer* resided in Chapman but never shot at anyone. There were *Broadaxes* at Wichita and Coffeyville and a *Broadax* at Howard, but the editors were no more gifted in removing cuticle than were the *Scalping Knife*, the *Korn Knife*, or the *Astonisher*.

The *Tomahawk* lived at Cullison, the *Kicker* at Circleville,

88

the *Mallet* at Mullinville, and the *Boomerang* at Beattie, but not one of them came anywhere near living up to its name.

It might be expected that the *Hornets* at Artesia and Spring-lake, the *Wasp* at Netawaka, the *Flame* at Narka, the *Scorcher* at Grigsby, the *Gas Jet* at Elmdale, the *Eye Opener* at Parsons, the *Fire Brand* at Clay Center, the *Mustard Seed* at Ottawa, and the *Calcium Light* at Belleville would have a good deal to say about men and affairs. But Sol Miller of the *Kansas Chief*, Dan Anthony at Leavenworth, and a dozen other editors packed more wallop in a sentence than the editors of these papers could muster in a column.

The editors who used the names of their towns as a part of the name for their newspapers appear to have fared somewhat better. There was the *Cashier* at Cash City, the *Obelisk* at Monument, the *Thomas County Cat* at Colby, the *Wideawake* at Wakefield, and the *Saw* at Sawyer. The *Border Ruffian*, a newspaper on the eastern border of Kansas in the early days, bobbed up some forty years later at Coolidge, four hundred miles from the original habitat. There was the *Prairie Owl* at Fargo Springs and the *Prairie Dog* at Lake City; the *Coyote* was published at Scott City. The *Infant Wonder* at Parsons never emerged from swaddling clothes, and the *Dunlap Sweet Chariot* was not sweet and did not have workable running gears. The *Little Sand Pounder* was published at Abilene. The *Cyclone* was issued once at Ellsworth and for four years at Cherokee. The *B-B-Blizzard* at Kingsley was another one-issue paper, published by the passengers on a Santa Fé passenger train stranded in the town during a blizzard. The *Kansas Sod House* lived for a short time at Ravanna, as did the *Rag Baby* at Kirwin. The *Kansas Cowboy* was published at Dodge City during the days when that town stepped out in lurid colors as the cowboy capital. Conductor, a town in western Kansas, chose the appropriate name *Conductor Punch* for its newspaper. *Bundle of Sticks* was published at Garden City, and the *Loco Motive* was the official paper in Loco, Finney County.

The new towns were not alone in devising funny names for their papers. Sometimes the older towns furnished a laugh or two in the same manner, though the papers followed the normal pattern of a country weekly, with patent insides, local news and correspondence, and occasionally a few editorial fulminations. In this category may be listed the *Birch Rod*, the *Fanatic*, the *Spoiled Child*, the *Miniature*, and the *Convincer* at Emporia. At Topeka were published *Knocker*, *Ham and Eggs*, *Ark Light*, *Chips*, *Centennial Tea Chest*, *Fire and Banner*, *Golf Bag*, *Hurry Kain*, *Ginger Snap*, *Pink Rag*, *Push*, *Saturday Night Wheeze*, *Lantern*, *Pilgrim*, *Shawnee Drumbeat*, *Tattler*, *Tramp*, and *That Tired Feeling*. Carry Nation and her friends published the *Smasher's Mail* in Topeka for several years.

The *Silver Cause* had quite a circulation in Wichita during the days of the Free Silver Movement. The *Blaze*, *Grit*, *Sunday Growler*, *Jibber Jab*, and *Arrow* were also published in Wichita.

The *Rose of Sharon* lived at Sharon Springs; the *Rays of Light* at McPherson; the *Inkelinger's Advertiser* at Westmoreland; the *Crank* at Geuda Springs; the *Mocking Bird* at nearby Oxford; the *Mirage* at Cassoday; the *Lyre* at Louisville; and *Lucifer the Light Bearer* at Valley Falls and later at Topeka.

An editor named Patrick lived at Valley Falls for three weeks, during which time his weekly newspaper had three different names: *Patrick's Paralyzer*, *Patrick's Independent*, and *Patrick's Advertiser*.

The *Prophet* was published at Harper and the *Question Mark* at Columbus, while at Fort Scott the editor picked the name *Sasnak* (Kansas spelled backwards) for his newspaper. The *Torch of Liberty* was published at Mound City; the *New Age* at Topeka; the *New Idea* at Clifton; the *New Man* at Beloit; and the *New Leaf* at Lane. The *Effingham New Leaf* has been published at Effingham since 1894. The *Cap Sheaf* at Grainfield is one of the older papers in western Kansas.

The *Boomer* was published at Ryanville and at Kendall, and the *Rising Sun* appeared at Salina. The *Sprig of Myrtle* was published by one of the secret societies for some years. The *Smelter* was published at Pittsburg, and the *Terry Eye* was the Finney County paper. The *Bison Bee* and the Ludell *Wildcat* were active little papers, and the *Dark Horse* was published in Sherman County for a short time. The *Rustler* was published at Wano, in Cheyenne County; the *Cosmos* at Council Grove; the *Irrigator* at Garden City; the *Light* at Liberty; the *Kendall Ken* at Kendall; the *Postal Card* at Wellington; the *Echo* at Fall River; and the *Kansas Cultivator* at Garden City. The *Western Cyclone* was a Negro publication at Nicodemus, and the *Frontiersman* was published at Bird City.

The fact that most of these newspapers did not live up to expectations, or failed to produce the fire their names foretold, may be the cause for their early demise. The editors whose papers survived were often more vitriolic and stirred up more trouble than the lads with the fancy names. Kansas editors were called upon to fight crooked politicians from the very beginning, and it may be noted that in its first fifteen years of statehood Kansas had five impeachments, in the course of which two state officers were convicted, one was acquitted, and two resigned before they could be brought to trial. In that same period two United States senators were removed from office because of the illegal use of money during their elections.

The result of this vigilance on the part of Kansas newspapermen has been a state signally free from scandals in its official families. There are occasional outbreaks, but Kansas editors have taken great pains to watch over the activities and methods of public officials. Not one has ever shown fear of any political leader who was inclined to misuse public confidence.

As has been ably indicated by others, the spirit of Kansas is (or has been) singularly Puritan despite the apparent ebullience of its founders and many of its notable citizens. Kansas editors have had extraordinary faith in themselves, and having this they are individualists. The combination of these two traits spells terror to the unholy in high places. In a sense, this is a survival from a 'former age, a reincarnation of the frontier, which in the past has been indulgent of minor vices but quickly outraged by the major ones. Modern industrial society, close-packed in some geographical areas, seems to see sin through the other end of the telescope.

16: *Miles of Stone Fence Posts*

A N UNUSUAL feature of the landscape in central and western Kansas is the series of stone fence posts that may be seen over an area of twelve or fourteen counties. These posts were often quarried on the farms where they were set, and at one time many quarries handled this particular stone as a commercial product.

It has been estimated that there are between thirty and forty thousand miles of stone fence posts in Kansas. In Ness and Hodgeman counties alone the Kansas Geological Survey found more than three thousand miles of the posts. In adjoining counties the rock used in the posts may be found near the surface, and farmers have been known to haul the rock for many miles in an area where there was no suitable timber and wooden posts were far too expensive.

German-Russian settlers in Ellis, Rush, Russell, and nearby counties are said to have been the first to use stone fence posts. In most instances these farmers, who were generally living in sod shanties or dugouts, were too poor to buy wooden posts. The stone fence-post rock has also been used extensively in the region in public buildings, county courthouses, city halls, churches, and many business structures.

Some Kansas "Frankensteins"
(*left to right*) Bill Shiftless, Maybelle Gaddy, Ima Washout, Drake Watson, and Abner Handy

The rock is composed of the upper layer of the Greenhorn limestone formation, which outcrops in more than a dozen counties in north-central and western Kansas, extending from the western border of Washington County across Hodgeman County. Often the outcrop occurs near the surface, ranging from one to five feet beneath the topsoil. The strata varies from six to ten inches in thickness, and where it is covered by a thick layer of soil it is quite soft and somewhat chalky and therefore easily quarried. The rock has a median line of iron one to two inches wide, which was deposited when the limestone was being formed. It is this median line which gives the stone its unusual appearance. The rock is gray when first quarried but turns a yellowish-gray color when exposed to the air.

There are two rather crude but effective methods of quarrying the stone. One method, which is employed throughout the year, consists of pinching off the stone in wedges of a specified size, depending on whether the stone is to be used for posts or in construction. When the overburden is removed, holes are made in the rock every two or three feet with hand drills. Then wedges are driven into these holes, and the posts are pinched off.

By the second method, the posts could be quarried during the winter months when farm work was slack. After the overburden was removed, a line of holes was drilled in the rock all along the outcrop. These holes were then filled with water, and the first hard freeze finished the work for the farmer. All he had to do was drill a hole according to the length of the fence post desired and fill it with water. Or he could cut the ledge of rock into whatever length he needed by drilling holes at the proper distances and allowing the freezing process to cut his posts into the desired lengths.

The Kansas Geological Survey calculated the value of the stone fence posts in Ness and Hodgeman counties to exceed $750,000. The value of the stone used in public buildings, business structures, and residences exceeded a million dollars.

The fence wires are fastened to the stone posts by means of notches or drilled holes. Barbed wire is fastened in the notches by a band of smooth wire so that the wires are maintained at equal distances. Two or three strands usually make up a fence, depending on the animals kept on the particular farm.

Although fence-post quarrying has almost ceased today, there is still some quarrying for buildings. The rock has also been split at the median streak, cut and polished, and used for decorative purposes and flagstones. Farmers can still obtain stone posts as replacements, and one may still see a few stone telephone poles two and three times as long as the ordinary fence posts.

Geologists have noted that the fence-post rock contains relatively few fossils, while other limestone deposits in the same region are full of fossils of all sizes and many shapes. Just why this upper strata of the Greenhorn limestone formation should be practically free of fossils has never been satisfactorily explained.

17: *Walking Cattle to Market*

DURING the days when the railroads were pushing across the state to meet the cattle trails, five towns were especially noted as railheads: Abilene, Ellsworth, Wichita, Newton, and Dodge City.

Ellsworth and Newton were generally regarded as the roughest of the five, but the other three were plenty tough by any standards, and all of them had much of the romantic as well as the lurid when the cowboys came to town to end the long trek across the prairies and the isolation from female

94

society. The craving for liquor and the tender touch of a woman was amply satisfied in the cow towns. When the cowboys were broke or the town marshals had wearied of their goings-on, they indulged in one last glorious fling and departed, to seek again the cattle barons and the herds of lowing kine.

Possibly one other town should be added to the list. Baxter Springs in southeast Kansas, was the end of the trail for some cowboys and cattle owners. It was never so rough as the other towns, and only a comparatively small quantity of cattle was handled there. But Baxter Springs has a story to tell.

At the close of the Civil War there was no market for vast numbers of Texas longhorns. The South lacked the funds to buy cattle, and there were so few ships moving to and from the Gulf ports that few cattle could be transported by water to northern markets. Also, transport by water was unsatisfactory because of the absence of corn and hay to fatten the animals.

A few cattlemen hit upon the idea of driving their cattle northeast to the western terminal of the Missouri Pacific at Sedalia, Missouri. A few hundred head were driven by this route, and the experiment was successful for about a year. Then native Missouri cattle began to break out with so-called Texas fever, a disease spread by ticks. The poor Missouri farmers were hit hard by the loss of the few milk cows they owned, and they determined to stop the drive across their area. Armed with squirrel rifles and shotguns, they came down to the state line, and while they did not erect signs reading "They Shall Not Pass," their patrols along the border stopped the movement of cattle to Sedalia. Thus Baxter Springs became the terminal of the Okmulgee Trail.

The cattlemen sold their cattle to any Kansan who would buy. Some of them sent their herds on north over the fort-to-fort highway to Kansas City and St. Joseph, where the animals could be loaded on the Burlington railroad or shipped by steamboat to the eastern corn country. Many cattle were sold to Iowa farmers who had a surplus of corn. But farmers in Iowa and Illinois soon lost their enthusiasm for the longhorns when native cattle began to come down with Texas fever.

Each of the other five Kansas towns have been designated at one time or other as the end of the Chisholm Trail. As a matter of fact, only Wichita should be listed as the northern terminal of the trail. Dodge City and Ellsworth generally handled cattle brought up from Texas on other trails.

The true Chisholm Trail extended south from Wichita, across the Cherokee Strip, and through the Indian Territory to the Canadian River, west of present Oklahoma City. Jesse Chisholm, a half-blood Cherokee, and James R. Mead, a well-known trader, traveler, and explorer in Kansas, entered into an agreement whereby Chisholm established one trading post on the present site of Wichita and another on the Canadian River, between Oklahoma City and Fort Reno. At that time Mead was transporting merchandise from the East for sale to the Indians and returning with hides and other goods the Indians had to sell. Chisholm made regular trips between the two posts, and his teams and wagons soon defined the trail. Since he avoided hills and bluffs and crossed the Arkansas, the Chikaskia, the Salt Fork, and other streams at shallow points, his trail followed a somewhat circuitous route.

Immediately after the close of the Civil War the laws of supply and demand brought about an increasing need for cattle in the corn-producing areas. Texas had cattle in abundance but lacked transportation facilities. This circumstance gave rise to the well-known comment that a cattleman's poverty was determined by his investment in cattle.

J. G. McCoy, an Illinois farmer and stockman, came west in the hopes of obtaining cattle. In Abilene he soon learned that transportation difficulties made it practically impossible to secure any sizeable quantity of cattle from Texas. But McCoy put his resources and energy to work and set about solving the problem. First, he negotiated with railroad officials to construct a hotel and extensive stockyards in Abilene. Then he visited several of the Texas cattle barons and sent emissaries to others to tell them of the market at Abilene. The cattlemen were enthusiastic about the new market but objected to traveling hundreds of miles across trackless prairies. McCoy then told them of Chisholm's post on the Canadian River and the well-marked trail to the trading post at the junction of the Little Arkansas and the Big Arkansas. From there, McCoy promised to plow a furrow which the cattlemen could follow to Abilene. With this assurance of guidance, the cattlemen soon eagerly accepted the proposal. A similar movement of cattle had taken place in 1859, when John C. Dawson moved a herd north to the present site of Denver, Colorado.

Thus began a practice which was to continue in Kansas for some fifteen years. Abilene and Ellsworth reigned as the cowboy capitals on the Kansas Pacific line, until the Atchison, Topeka, and Santa Fé wedged its rails between the cattle country and the northern rail line. Then Wichita, Newton, and Dodge City succeeded to the title.

It was necessary that the cattle have water and feed on the long trek. Furthermore, the animals must be in fair condition when they arrived at the railhead, if they were to catch the eye of eastern buyers. These conditions were not always satisfactorily fulfilled, but the movement of animals to these Kansas railheads in the years after the Civil War supplied millions of pounds of edible if not prime beef to meat-hungry northern populations.

The first shipment of cattle from Abilene consisted of twenty carloads, which were billed to Chicago and left Abilene on September 5, 1867. Before winter closed in, some 35,000 head of cattle had been shipped from the Abilene yards.

Estimates of the total number of cattle moved to Kansas markets in this fashion have ranged as high as fifteen to twenty million head. However, the most reliable figures now available would indicate the total to be somewhere between five and seven million head. The government census of 1880 presented an extensive array of figures on shipments during the period 1867–80:

For Sedalia, Missouri	
1866	260,000[1]
For Abilene, Kansas	
1867	35,000
1868	75,000
1869	350,000
1870	300,000
1871	700,000
For Wichita and Ellsworth, Kansas	
1872	350,000
1873	405,000
1874	166,000
1875	151,618
For Dodge City, Kansas	
1876	322,000
1877	201,159
1878	265,646
1879	257,927
1880 (including movement to Caldwell and Hunnewell)	384,497
Total cattle driven to 1880	4,223,847

In 1880, 164 herds of cattle, averaging 2,342 head, were driven northward. Thirty-three of these herds were moved on to the Northwest for breeding purposes. It was estimated that 2,000 men and 6,500 horses made the drive during that one year. The time required to make a drive varied from forty to seventy days, and twelve to fifteen miles were covered on a day's march. The cost for moving each animal averaged seventy-five cents a day.

[1] Most of these cattle never reached Sedalia because of the opposition at the Missouri border.

In 1883, 260,000 head of cattle were loaded at Dodge City. In December, 1883, the *Dodge City Times* stated that 3,400 carloads had been shipped during the season. In April, 1884, the *Dodge City Globe* predicted that herds arriving in Dodge City that season would total about 300,000 head.

The records show that during the days of the cattle drives herds were purchased on the range at six to ten dollars a head. When they reached their eastern destination, they brought sixty to eighty dollars a head, depending on bargaining power, not on weight, since purchases were seldom made on the basis of weight.

By 1868, when the great movement of Texas cattle was well under way, wheat was selling in St. Louis at $2.05 a bushel, white corn at $0.99, yellow corn at $0.95, and oats at $0.63. Pork was quoted at $29.00 a hundred pounds, and it may be assumed that beef prices were comparable.

In 1871 Archibald L. Williams, attorney general of Kansas, entered in his diary a payment of thirty dollars for a tailor-made suit. His hired girl received two dollars a week. At about the same time a Texas cow hand or a Kansas farm hand was getting eighteen to twenty dollars a month and "found" (room and board). In the early nineties maids could be hired for two and three dollars a week, and a hired man received twelve to eighteen dollars a month for year-round work. The daily stipend was one or two dollars a day, depending on the skill of the laborer.

So much fact and fiction has been written about the exploits of the cowboys and the efforts of Wild Bill Hickok, Wyatt Earp, Bat Masterson, and other lawmen to tame the cow towns that no good purpose would be served in retelling them here. Among the many worthy accounts, McCoy's book especially reveals a conscious effort to tell the unvarnished truth. I feel that his *Historic Sketches of the Cattle Trade and the Southwest* (Kansas City, Missouri, 1874) is indispensable. Floyd B. Streeter of Hays has written an excellent history of the period,[2] and Robert M. Wright, who had first-hand knowledge, presented a factual account of the days when the cattle trail ended at Dodge City.[3] Sam P. Ridings has written an extended history of the Chisholm Trail, including descriptions of the colorful personalities and outstanding events which characterized the old trail days.[4] Edward Everett Dale[5] and E. S. Osgood[6] have written extensively upon the cattle industry before 1900 and men who made it what it was. Stanley Vestal has just published a masterly account of the rip-snorting days in Dodge City which must take its place among the best accounts of the period 1872–86.[7]

From the range and extensiveness of these works of authorship it must be clear that Kansas has played an interesting role in the cattle trade of the middle part of America. The romantic chapter has been closed, only to be succeeded in our time by an industry vaster, more scientific, and almost as exciting as the droving days of the past, extending from the priceless Flint Hills of eastern Kansas to the high plains in the west. Steers don't walk as far today, a cattleman will tell you, but they grow a lot fatter.

[2] *Prairie Trails and Cow Towns* (Boston, Chapman and Grimes, 1936).

[3] *Dodge City, the Cowboy Capital* (Wichita, Wichita Eagle, 1913).

[4] *The Chisholm Trail* (Guthrie, Oklahoma, Co-operative Publishing Company, 1936).

[5] *The Range Cattle Industry* (Norman, University of Oklahoma Press, 1930).

[6] *The Day of the Cattleman* (Minneapolis, University of Minnesota Press, 1929).

[7] *Queen of the Cowtowns: Dodge City, 1872–1886* (New York, Harper and Brothers, 1952).

1 8: *Setting the Railroad Pattern*

ONE OF the most significant meetings ever held in Kansas Territory was the Railroad Convention of 1860, which met to develop a plan for the construction of land-grant railroads. The convention reached an agreement on the companies to be granted land subsidies and established the permanent railroad pattern of Kansas.

The convention was called, directed, and controlled by the most influential men of the territory, who had the power to parcel out the subsidies and enforce the decrees of the convention.

When Kansas was opened to settlement, there were only three available means of transportation. One could travel on foot, on horseback, or by river steamboat. However, since the Missouri Pacific Railroad was building west of St. Louis, and the Hannibal and St. Joseph (now the Burlington) was making progress on the railway connecting those two cities, it was only a matter of time before Kansas would begin to follow suit.

The first territorial legislature, which convened in Kansas in March, 1855, had granted charters to five railroads in Kansas —a worthy first effort, despite the fact that the charters were granted by a "bogus legislature." The railroads thus incorporated were the Central Railroad, which was to extend from some point on the Missouri River to some point on the western border of the territory; the South Kansas, from some point on the eastern border directly west of Springfield, Missouri, to some point on the western border; the Leavenworth, Pawnee and Western, from a point near Leavenworth on the west bank of the Missouri River to Pawnee, Fort Riley, and westward; the Leavenworth and Lecompton, to connect the two cities; and the Kansas Valley, from the south bank of the Kansas River, at a point near the mouth of the river, westward to Pawnee.

At every session of the territorial legislature until 1860 at least a dozen railroads were granted charters. Every townsite promoter became a railroad promoter as well, fully realizing that if he could persuade a railroad to indicate even a slight interest in his town, the speculative value of his town lots would rise rapidly.

The people who came to Kansas in the early days were well aware of the transportation difficulties they would have to face. In the new territory, only recently wrested from the Indians, there were no roads, no ferries, no bridges. The one compensating feature was the plains area itself, which was easy to cross and provided ample room for maneuvering around escarpments and other obstacles. The Santa Fe Trail, the Oregon Trail, and the military roads from Fort Leavenworth to Fort Riley, Fort Scott, and Fort Gibson in Oklahoma were the only clearly defined highways in the area.

When the Missourians closed the Missouri River to antislavery passengers and freight, the only transportation available to pioneers from the North was the route Jim Lane had recommended in his speeches in Chicago and other eastern cities: to the railhead at Iowa City, then along the Lane Trail across Iowa to Nebraska City, Nebraska, and from there south to Topeka.

It has often been said that in the years 1855–60 "paper railways" became more common in Kansas than weeds in a roadside ditch. By 1860 more than one hundred railroads had been incorporated by the territorial legislature, and promoters were pulling every string at their command to secure approval for their lines.

About this time the *Atchison Champion* sounded its call to arms. The leading citizens of the territory, possessed of a loyalty and patriotism rare in political conflicts, wanted to see Kansas grow and prosper. They realized clearly that the multiplicity

of proposed lines would impede the development of a successful railroad system. John A. Martin, the editor of the *Atchison
Champion,* had this to say:

Let us act like men who have the good of the whole territory more
at heart than the success of a few little dirt-eating paper cities. Let
us endeavor to obtain harmony and united action by conciliation
and united desire for the general good.

This statesmanlike declaration was to embody the spirit of
the Railroad Convention. Martin, Edmund G. Ross, editor of
the *Topeka Record* and later famous as the senator who cast
the vote acquitting President Andrew Johnson of impeachment
charges, and Cyrus K. Holliday, founder of Topeka and the
incorporator of the Atchison and Topeka Railroad, conferred
many times about the situation. The result of their conversa-
tions was the calling of the Railroad Convention, to be held in
Topeka on October 17, 1860. The purpose of the convention
was to set a railroad pattern for Kansas which would offer the
greatest convenience to the largest number of inhabitants and
at the same time contribute to the growth and development of
the territory.

To the convention came 150 accredited delegates from
nineteen counties. Samuel C. Pomeroy of Atchison was elected
chairman. As soon as the temporary committees were selected,
difficulties over apportionment of votes threatened to wreck
the unity established by the promoters of the convention. Many
delegates wanted an apportionment based on the population in
each county. By this method the larger counties would, of
course, control the convention. The commercial interests in
the larger towns were also demanding an unequal voting power.
When the apportionment committee declared against an allotment based on population and gave each county equal voting
power, the entire Leavenworth delegation and three members
of the delegation from Douglas County withdrew. Thomas
Means of Leavenworth asserted that the delegates from the

western counties represented only "prairie sod." B. F. String-fellow of Atchison, editor and former attorney general of Missouri, replied that the day was not far off when those counties would have large populations, with improved farms, furnishing trainloads of produce for the markets of the world, that it should be in the interest of his (Means's) city to aid in building railroads to all parts of the territory to transport the products of the soil, to enable her, in fact, to become a metropolis of the territory. He added that it was business that made a metropolis, not the effort to destroy the very region that furnished the necessary articles of commerce.

But the Leavenworth and Douglas County members were not to be convinced. After their withdrawal, the convention appointed a committee composed of one member from each county to draft a proposal for railroad aid. (It may be noted here that political differences were tossed out of the convention. Stringfellow was an ardent advocate of slavery and the editor of a proslavery paper. Many other delegates also supported the slavery cause, while the three planners of the convention, Martin, Ross, and Holliday, and many others were antislavery. Yet throughout the convention there was not a single mention of political differences.) The report of the committee made the following recommendations:

That a memorial be presented to the Congress asking an appropriation of public lands to aid in the construction of the following railroads in Kansas:

First, A railroad from the western boundary of the state of Missouri where the Osage Valley and Southern Kansas terminates, westwardly, by the way of Emporia, Fremont and Council Grove, to the Fort Riley military reservation.

Second, A railroad from the city of Wyandotte [Kansas City, Kansas] connecting with the P.G.R. and the Pacific railroad, up the Kansas valley, by way of Lawrence, Lecompton, Tecumseh, Manhattan and the Fort Riley military reservation, to the western boundary of the territory.

Third, A railroad running from Lawrence to the southern boundary of Kansas, in the direction of Fort Gibson and Galveston Bay.

Fourth, A railroad running from Atchison, by way of Topeka, through the territory in the direction of Santa Fé.

Fifth, A railroad running from Atchison to the western boundary of Kansas.[1]

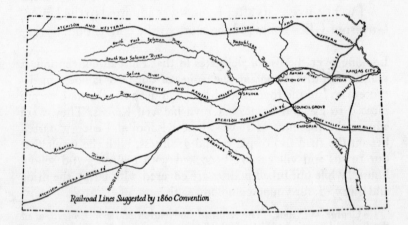

Railroad Lines Suggested by 1860 Convention

Of the five proposals, only the first remained uncompleted. However, the section from Emporia northwest to Council Grove and Fort Riley was built and became a part of the Missouri, Kansas and Texas lines from Parsons to Fort Riley. The eastern section of the projected line is approximately the line of the Missouri Pacific through central Kansas. The line was never completed, largely because it was not energetically promoted until after the practice of making land subsidies had ceased.

[1] From Proceedings published in the *Atchison Freedom's Champion* (October 22, 1860).

105

The delegates were directed to secure petitions from the citizens in their counties asking that these lines be the only ones recognized by Congress. Then a committee of five was named to present the petition to Congress and see to it that members of Congress from Kansas support the petition. When Kansas became a state, the senators and representatives sent to Congress were urged to observe the pattern set by the convention. They agreed to do so, and in declining to support other projects, they were assured adequate claims for land grants for the five lines.

Twenty-five years after Kansas was admitted to the Union, Governor Glick appraised the work of the convention:

Looking over the list of delegates in that railroad convention, it will be seen that it contains the names of our most eminent men—those who laid the foundation broad and deep for the state we are pleased to call our home, our own beloved Kansas. They were among the foremost of those whose wisdom and energy started her on the road to prosperity and greatness, with the result that our towns and villages are bedecked with churches and school houses, while our broad prairies are covered with farms, the pride and glory of our young commonwealth.[2]

[2] George W. Glick, "The Railroad Convention of 1860," *Collections* of the Kansas Historical Society, Vol. IX, 497.

III. *The Stuff It's Made of*

Driving Cattle to Market

19: *Kansas, Jayhawk, and Jayhawker*

THE JAYHAWK is a fearsome bird—if, indeed, it is a bird. So many pictures and descriptions of the Jayhawk have been published that it is difficult to describe the species adequately to a non-Kansan.

The dictionaries do not recognize the existence of the Jayhawk, though they include "Jayhawker." Webster defines the latter as "a member of a band of guerrilas, originally antislavery men, especially in Kansas and Missouri, before and during the Civil War; hence, an irregular soldier."

A few years ago Kansas school children read in a supplement to their geography book that the word came from the name of a bird native to the locality. That statement set the children on ornithologists, fossil collectors, and Audubon societies. "Show us the bird, or the bones or the feathers or something," demanded the children. The ornithologists and the fossil collectors could only hang their heads in shame and admit there was no such bird.

The late John J. Ingalls, one of the most trenchant satirists Kansas has ever known, wrote on the subject:

The Audubon of the 20th century, as he compiles the history of the birds of Kansas, will vainly search the ornithological biographies of his illustrious predecessors for any allusion to the jay-hawk. Investigation will disclose the jay and the hawk; the former a mischievous, quarrelsome egg-sucker, a blue-coated cousin of the crow and an epicure of carrion; the latter a cloud-hunting pirate, the assassin of the atmosphere, whose flattened skull and rapacious beak, and insatiable appetite for blood impel it to an agency of destruction and place it among the repulsive ranks of the living ministers of death. Were it not that nature forbids the adulterous confusion of her types, he might surmise that the jayhawk was a mule among birds, the illicit offspring of some sudden liaison or aerial intrigue, endowed with the most malign attributes of its progenitors.

But this conclusion would be unerringly rejected by the deductions of his science, he would be compelled to look elsewhere for this obscure tenant of the air, whose notable exploits caused it to be accepted as a symbol of the infant state, given to a famous regiment its title and to the inhabitants their novel appellation of Jayhawkers, by what happy nomenclature which would induce the unsophisticated chronicler to suppose that the population of Illinois was composed entirely of infants at the breast and that the chief vegetable productions of Missouri were ipecac and lobelia.[1]

Kirke Mechem, secretary of the Kansas Historical Society and collector of Jayhawk folklore, wrote that the bird was in the habit of flying backwards, "because he didn't care more than a whoop or two where he was going but wanted to know all about where he had been."

"The Jayhawk is peculiarly an expression of the spirit of Kansas," continued Mechem. "Like the state, it was born in adversity and its flight is to the stars. It is a fighting bird, full of the tough humor of the Territorial soldiers who first made it their mascot. A famous regiment of the Civil War was proud to bear its name. . . .

"The Jayhawk is a heroic bird, but don't try to treat it like a hero! You might receive a faint swoosh from its exhaust. It is

[1] "The Last of the Jayhawkers," *Kansas Magazine*, Vol. I, No. 4 (1872), 356.

a bird of peace. It is sentimental, and loves to croon strange words to itself at dawn or in a prairie twilight. Poetic words about ripening wheat, and prohibition, and service flags in the windows of quiet homes, and the purification of politics. Yes, the Jayhawk is heroic, but its heroism was bred in the courage of peace. The courage of a bird that can fly backwards into a dust storm squawking prosperity."[2]

Mary B. Rondeau composed a poem characterizing the bird in much the same manner:

> *I'm a Kansas Jayhawk,*
> *I'm a curious bird.*
> *I never have been seen,*
> *I never have been heard.*
> *I am just a Kansas myth,*
> *Dear to Kansas hearts,*
> *Guardian angel of the state—*
> *Whenever danger starts.*
> *I am a fighting Jayhawk,*
> *Fierce and cocky too,*
> *I look after Kansas folks*
> *No matter what they do.*
> *I'm a Kansas Jayhawk,*
> *I'm a curious bird.*
> *And you can just believe of me*
> *All you've ever heard.*[3]

Among Kansans there is a general belief, as yet unconfirmed, that the term Jayhawk is of Irish origin. A letter to Irish authorities brought the reply that, while the name might exist in some isolated locality, it was also possible that the proponent of the theory had "an inventive turn of mind." Again quoting from Mr. Mechem:

[2] *The Mythical Jayhawk* (Kansas State Historical Society, 1944).
[3] Published in *The Kansas City Star*, February 18, 1945.

The story of Pat Devlin has always encouraged the hope . . . that somewhere the bird had a prototype. Devlin was a native of Ireland, an early immigrant to Kansas. One day in 1856 he was returning home after some private plundering across the Missouri border. When asked what he had been up to, he replied, "You know, in Ireland we have a bird called the Jayhawk, which makes its living off of other birds. I guess you might say I have been Jayhawking."

The late Frank W. Blackmar, a professor at the University of Kansas for many years, wrote extensively of the Jayhawk and how it came to be attached to Kansas:

The "Jayhawk" is a myth. It has no historical origin but has had a historical use. It is neither beast, fish nor fowl. The myth had its rise in the characters of two birds that frequent the Missouri Valley, namely the blue jay, a noisy, quarrelsome, robber that takes delight in pouncing upon smaller birds and robbing their nests of eggs and young birds, and the sparrow hawk, a genteel killer of birds, rats, mice and rabbits, and, when necessary, a courageous and cautious fighter. Just when, where, and by whom the names of the two birds were joined in Jayhawk and applied to human beings, no one knows. However, it is known that the term "jayhawk" originated in the home territory of these birds somewhere between Texas and Nebraska. It is known that it was applied to an overland company of gold-seekers on their way through Nebraska to California. It was applied to Jennison's band of freebooters, to Montgomery's rangers, to Missouri guerrilla bands of border ruffians, and finally in a general way to the free soldiers of Kansas.

In the early days of uncertainty of government, life, and property, wherever bands were organized, requiring purpose, courage, boldness, and reckless daring, they were always candidates for the name either through choice or through the derision or the hatred of enemies. It is significant, also that "jayhawking" became a general term to express marauding or plundering.

It is not known how the name gradually became applied to all residents of Kansas. Perhaps it was because Kansas was nationally known as the center of disturbance and jayhawk became a nationally known byword. Probably Jennison's band of fighters and free-booters followed historically by Jennison's "Jayhawk regiment" in the Civil war had something to do with causing the name to adhere to Kansas. But Kansans accepted the totemic appellation with good grace and every loyal Kansan is proud to be a member of the Clan Kansas that now stands for nobler things than "jay-hawking."

The "Jayhawk" myth has become a spirit of progress and power. Gone has the spirit of robber birds; gone the reckless spirit of the lawless and disorderly bands of the stress and storm period. Only the spirit of comradeship and the courageous fighting qualities to make and keep Kansas free, remain. The spirit of the modern Jayhawk is to make Kansas great and strong and noble in good deeds. It is a benevolent spirit.

Kansas University seized the word as a shibboleth and attached it to the soil with "rock chalk" and brought out the K.U. yell, the greatest lung developer of all time. It is the voice of the clan. It is a call to comradeship through learning and righteousness.

The artists have tried to express the mythical bird in clever totemic designs, which range all the way from a "dicky-bird" with a huge bill, wearing boots, to a disconsolate crow, and to a fierce-looking fighting bird. All very well as a totem of the clan to express unity and loyalty, but the spirit of the Jayhawk refuses to be photographed.[4]

The early application of "Jayhawk" to Kansans is discussed in an article by William A. Lyman:

As to the origin of the name "Jayhawker" there seems to be some difference of opinion. Adj. Gen. S. M. Fox, in his story of the Seventh Kansas, says "the predatory habits of the jayhawk would indicate that the name as applied to Jennison's men was singularly appropriate." Ingalls wrote an essay on the "Last of the Jayhawkers," a title suggested, no doubt, by Cooper's *The Last of the Mohicans.* In it he gives a sketch of the career of Captain Cleveland,

[4] *Kansas* (Chicago, Standard Publishing Company, 1912).

and incidentally states that the jayhawk is a bird entirely unknown
to the ornithologist; that it is a myth. It is well known that the
name did not originate in Kansas, for as early as 1849 a party of
Argonauts from Illinois made the overland journey to California
and called themselves "Jayhawkers."[5]

In the spring of 1859, C. R. Jennison appeared at Mound
City from Monroe, Wisconsin. Being a man of spirit, and
possessed of certain qualities of leadership, he affiliated with the
Jayhawkers and soon became one of their officers. When the
border disputes began to quiet down, he organized and conducted "retaliatory" raids into Missouri.

With the coming of summer a movement spread to "clean
out nests of unclean birds," the "unclean birds" being proslavery sympathizers who were accused of harboring border
ruffians and furnishing them with information about free-
state settlers. In the process of ridding the territory of these
men, several victims were shot or hanged without benefit of
trial. In the fall of 1859 Joseph Williams, one of the judges
appointed by Buchanan to serve in Kansas, came to Mound
City to hold court. The lawless conditions he found there soon
convinced him that he was in personal danger. Hastily he adjourned his court and fled to St. Louis, reporting to the governor of Missouri and the federal authorities that his court had
been broken up by the Jayhawkers, that his life had been
threatened, and that a general condition of anarchy existed in
Linn County. The Missouri militia was called out and stationed
along the border, but the disturbance proved to lie primarily
in the judge's fevered imagination. Neither he nor his court
had been in the least danger. Meanwhile, troops from Fort
Riley and Fort Leavenworth were dispatched to the scene to
annihilate the little band of Jayhawkers. They surrounded
Jennison's home but after a diligent search failed to find him.
Cavalry and artillery were sent to Montgomery's fort a few
miles west of town. There, too, they found no one. The Jay-

5 *Collections* of the Kansas Historical Society.

hawkers had disappeared like the mist before the morning sun.

About the time of the beginning of hostilities in 1861, Captain Marshall Cleveland, a fugitive from the Missouri penitentiary, appeared in Mound City and soon became one of the leaders of the Jayhawkers. No defense can be made of the Jayhawkers' activities during this time. The damage they inflicted on proslavery Missourians ranged from robbery to murder and made the name Jayhawker a term of opprobrium and reproach.

In late August, 1861, Governor Robinson gave Jennison the authority to raise a regiment of cavalry. Placards were immediately posted in every village, announcing the "Independent Mounted Kansas Jayhawkers." The regiment, consisting of ten companies, was finally organized on October 28, 1861. Until the spring of 1862 it was known as the First Kansas Cavalry. Later, when Kansas regiments were numbered consecutively, the Jayhawkers became the Seventh Kansas Regiment. However, the band retained its nickname throughout the war.

Some years ago the Kansas Board of Education declared that the appellation Jayhawker was obnoxious to the inhabitants of the state and decreed in all solemnity that no textbook using the term would be allowed in Kansas schools. By this action the board hoped to rid Kansans of a supposedly insulting nickname. The effect was just the opposite. It appears that no other act could have brought the Jayhawker into more repute and popularity than the action of the board. Kansas editors and citizens rose up in wrath, and newspapers outside the state took up arms in their behalf and produced ringing editorials supporting the Jayhawkers. The *Chicago News* wrote:

Jayhawker seemed appropriate for the Kansas partisans because they were aggressive and impudent in their guerilla tactics. They raided the nests of other species; they were vigorous in defense of their own. They were rugged; they were individualists; they made their voices heard. They have been pretty much that breed ever since. . . . Whatever the original connotation of Jayhawker may have been, successive generations of Kansans have made it a badge of distinction. When Kansans cease to take pride in being Jayhawkers we have reached a sorry status. It would be a calamity.

Henry Malloy, illustrator of the *Daily Kansan* at the University of Kansas, popularized a cartoon which is now generally accepted as an adequate picture of the benign and friendly nature of the Jayhawk. Milton Nigg, also of the university, rendered the Jayhawk in clay. Chester Shore, erstwhile Kansas editor, discussed the various artists' conceptions of the Jayhawk:

Hundreds of different birds have represented the jayhawk. Each artist had his own conception of it. It is long-legged, short-legged, long-beaked, short-beaked, friendly or fierce, with shoes or with claws, yellow-beaked or red-breaked, with topnot or topnotless, and overfed or underfed.[6]

The "K.U. Yell" is one of the most famous college yells in the country. When Kansans visit foreign lands and bear down on "Rock Chalk, Jayhawk, K.U.," the listeners know they have met a group that won't be shoved around.

The *Graduate Magazine* of the University of Kansas once declared: "The Jayhawk, though, of course, a myth, does stand as the symbol of the righteous struggle put up by the Kansas pioneers for the lofty cause of freedom."

It has been suggested that some Kansas poet should write a song about the Jayhawk, which isn't a bad idea—so important a bird in Kansas folklore is certainly entitled to have a few musical chirps to its credit.

During World War II a new Jayhawk appeared. His story was revealed by Lieutenant Colonel Lowell R. Whitla, maintenance officer for the Kansas National Guard:

The seagoing Jayhawk was found to be webfooted of the

[6] From University of Kansas *Graduate Magazine*, Vol. XXIV (December, 1925).

specie Sailgieriens, a tough and prolific old bird that produced numerous offspring of lesser size.

On the forward port and starboard sides of the U.S.S. Radon proudly stood a guardian Kansas Jayhawk of heroic proportions. He was eight feet high and wore the crimson and blue of a true Kansan. This particular Jayhawk was one of the old-timers and no longer a college boy. So, in place of the letters KU he carried an ordnance bomb under one wing and a very serviceable monkey wrench under the other wing.

The crew of the U.S.S. Radon was composed of some of the army's finest men, the majority ordnance men. They are technicians and curious about all phases of their equipment and especially the guardian Jayhawk. "A Bunch of Tough Old Birds," the crew became known. Their toughness and curiosity caused them to remove the Jayhawk's shoes and lo, and behold, they found him to be webfooted and with spurs.[7]

20. *The Kansas State Flower*

THE LATITUDE of Kansas—and its longitude, too, for that matter, between the foothills of the Rockies on the west and the rich lowlands of the Missouri on the east—makes it something more than a great agricultural state. For a variety of reasons, of which geographical location is one, but principally having to do with cloudless skies from early spring until the time of frost, the state is probably the greatest producer of sunflowers in North America.

The sunflower is, of course, the state flower. The question frequently asked, however, is, Why did the state pick a flower which is not indigenous to the area, as are the Kansas gayfeather and many other flowers recorded by early-day explorers, traders, and missionaries?

[7] *Kansas Historical Quarterly,* Vol. XV (1947), 320.

The late George P. Morehouse of Council Grove, state senator, author, poet, and for many years an active participant in state affairs, was primarily responsible for the selection of the sunflower. Strangely enough, the choice was made on a trip to Colorado Springs. Visitors to the summer resort from Kansas and Missouri had inaugurated weekly picnics and gatherings. At the first of these outings, the Missourians showed up proudly wearing badges reading, "You'll have to show me." No one had thought about a badge for the Kansans, but when the first contingent arrived at the park the next week, every visitor from Kansas was wearing a sunflower. Some enterprising Kansan had gone out into the Colorado fields and picked his state flower.

Senator Morehouse returned home to begin the campaign to choose the sunflower as the state flower. In the state senate he introduced the bill which finally became law in 1903: "That the Helianthus or wild native sunflower is hereby made, designated, and declared to be the state flower and floral emblem of Kansas."

In a preamble to the bill Senator Morehouse wrote:

Whereas, Kansas has a native wild flower common throughout her borders, hardy and conspicuous, of definite, unvarying and striking shape, easily sketched, molded, and carved, having armorial capacities, ideally adapted for artistic reproduction, with its strong, distinct disk and its golden circle of clear glowing rays —a flower that a child can draw on a slate, a woman can work in silk, or a man can carve on stone or fashion in clay; and

Whereas, This flower has to all Kansans a historic symbolism which speaks of frontier days, winding trails, pathless prairies, and is full of the life and glory of the past, the pride of the present, and richly emblematic of the majesty of a golden future, and is a flower which has given Kansas the world-wide name, "the Sunflower State."

There is no doubt that Senator Morehouse and his associates believed the wild sunflower, which grows rank through-out Kansas in the driest years and in the most unfavorable areas, to be a native flower. Not until some forty years later was this belief exploded.

In the *Kansas Guide* appears this statement:

The sunflower, curiously enough, is not native to Kansas. Its seeds came from the Southwest, in mud and dirt clinging to the broad wheels of freight wagons plying the Santa Fé Trail in early days. The small variety that grows wild along the roadside and in uncultivated fields is regarded as a pest, but varieties producing large seeds are cultivated for chicken feed.[1]

The Reverend John G. Pratt, early-day missionary to the Indians, first visited Kansas in 1837 and returned to settle on the Delaware Reservation (now Jefferson and Leavenworth counties). Many years later, he described his first view of the Kansas scene:

Leaving Boston in April with my wife, we reached the then territory May 14, being about four weeks in slow travel. The territory at that time was in perfect quiet, and a most beautiful country it was. My first look at a green open prairie on a sunny day seemed to be a look at the ocean, with which I was familiar, but this was "Flora" in her gayest attire; the eye was too limited in its capacity to take in such wide and far extending area of beauty —the like of which will never be seen again in Kansas. The coming of the settlers has spoiled all this. Though still the sunflower state, the earlier dress of nature was more comely, it was nature's beauty.[2]

State Representative J. W. Berryman of Ashland, a Kansas banker, farmer, and stockman, was the son of an early mission-ary and was himself a teacher at the old Shawnee mission for

[1] Federal Writers Project, *Kansas, A Guide to the Sunflower State* (New York, The Viking Press, 1939), 380.

[2] From a letter to Secretary Adams (preserved in Kansas Historical Society manuscript section).

several years. In an address before the Kansas Historical Society, Mr. Berryman described the southwestern grasslands:

Originally it was covered by a solid mat of close-curled buffalo grass which grew to the exclusion of any other vegetation. There were no weeds of any kind, and only on the lower or sandier grounds were there any other grasses. Here might be found, then as now, some admixture with bunch grasses, a dwarf variety of sage, a few yucca plants, and occasionally dwarfed shrubs of the mesquite variety, or sand plum. Practically all other vegetation throughout the region has come since the advent of the settler, and is foreign in nature.[3]

In many of the histories of the early days may be found notations to the effect that the sunflower came after the land was broken. "Whenever the land was broken up and the sod destroyed, as along the edge of the Santa Fé Trail, sunflowers grew up and flourished," wrote one settler. "As soon as the first sod cornfields were planted the farmers had to fight the sunflowers. Any farm land left uncultivated would raise sunflowers for a few years and then go back to buffalo grass."

L. A. Madison, a settler in southwest Kansas and a member of Congress from the old Seventh (now the Fifth) Congressional District, wrote, "The Santa Fé Trail is the historic birthplace of the sunflower."

But Hugh Powell, resident of Kansas for many years and editor of the *Coffeyville Journal*, takes exception to the assertions that the sunflower would not grow on the unbroken sod of the prairies. Mr. Powell taught school in Ness County, where each morning he gathered dry sunflower stalks as kindling to start the school fire. "During four summers of residence in Ness we many times saw sunflowers growing on unbroken ground," wrote Mr. Powell. "Don't let anybody try to make the reader believe that the writer hereof is trying to disparage

[3] *Collections* of the Kansas Historical Society, Vol. XVII, 563.

the choice of the sunflower as the state flower. The sunflower
is the most numerous flower of the state. It may not be a native,
but it is so associated with the Kansas landscape, it provides so
colorful a vision to native and visitor alike, that there should
be no quarrel with those who picked it for the state flower.
The Kansas gayfeather, while a native, is a most beautiful flower on the prairies but it does not grow everywhere in Kansas,
as does the sunflower. Chicago florists will pay five dollars a
hundred for the Kansas gayfeather but they won't pay a dime
a ton for the sunflowers. Even that is no argument against the
sunflower as a state flower."

When the Kansas National Guard adopted a bronze button
bearing the sunflower for the uniform of Kansas soldiers, Senator Morehouse addressed the guard at Fort Riley, paying elo-
quent tribute to the state's flower:

This native wild flower is common throughout our borders,
and is always hardy and conspicuous. It lifts its hardy head in
triumph along our most beautiful and classic valleys and mingles
its cheerful light in the verdure of expanding prairies. The seasons
have little effect on its coming, for it flourishes in time of flood and
the drouth of the arid summer adds to the multitude of its blossoms.
It is of definite, unvarying and striking shape, ever faithful, whether
gracing the beautiful gardens of the rich or lingering near the
humble habitation of the poor. Wherever reproduced, whether in
color or canvas, worked in iron or chiseled in stone or marble, its
identity is ever present.

It speaks eloquently of frontier days, when buds and blossoms
of civilization were not numerous and when we were deprived of
many of the refinements we now enjoy. The sunflower recalls
paths and winding trails, and we are reminded of its golden lines of
beauty, at times making their graceful turns over hill and vale, and
breaking the dull monotony of many a prairie scene. It is not a
blossom lingering a few brief hours, but lasts for a season. It grace-
fully nods to the caresses of the earliest morning zephyrs. Its
bright face greets the rising orb of day and faithfully follows him
in his onward course through the blazing noontime, till the pink-

tinted afterflow of sunset decorates the western sky and marks the quiet hour of eventide.[4]

In 1880 Noble L. Prentis, a Kansas editor and the author of a standard history of Kansas, wrote:

The Capitol square is surrounded by a dense growth, rods in width, of rampant sunflowers. They grow as big, rank and yellow as if they were forty miles from a house. The sunflower ought to be made the emblem of our state. Nothing checks it or kills it. It is always "happy as a big sunflower." Grasshoppers never held the edge on it; and in drouthy times when everything else wilts and throws up its hands, the sunflower continues business at the old stand. It probably has some private arrangement with nature for securing "aid."[5]

So far as can be ascertained, this was the first time the sunflower was suggested as the state emblem. In the old days the *Kansas Magazine* had often referred to the sunflower as rampant and beautiful, but none of the writers had gone on to suggest that it be made the state flower. It remained for Noble Prentis and, twenty years later, George P. Morehouse to make the idea an accomplished fact.

Claude M. Older of Hays has paid a lasting tribute to the sunflower and to the courage and hardihood of the people who chose it for their symbol:

The sunflower, in emulation of those Kansas pioneers, men and women, who, pitifully poor in worldly goods, but so enormously wealthy in spirit and stamina . . . stands alone expecting nothing of man and asking little of nature. He holds no brief for the quitter, enters no interpleader for the weakling. Drought, flood, blizzard or hot winds . . . he takes them as they come—fights

[4] "The Sunflower and the Law Making it the *Floral* Emblem of Kansas," *Kansas Magazine,* Vol. II, No. 3, 17.

[5] From the *Atchison Champion,* 1880.

them all, and having won, turns his face to the sun—ever upward, with a flaunt of his golden crown at puny menfolk riding by in their vaunted wisdom and borrowed splendor.

21: *We Have Led the Way*

MANY TIMES Kansas has led other states in adopting improved methods of government and promoting the welfare of the people. In 1922 William Allen White wrote:

Abolition, prohibition, Populism and the Bull Moose, the exit of the roller towel, the appearance of the bank guarantee, the blue sky law,—these things came popping out of Kansas like bats out of Hell. Sooner or later other states take up these things, and then Kansas goes on breeding other troubles. Kansas, fair, fat and 61 last month, is the nation's tenth muse, the muse of prophesy. There is just one way to stop progress in America; and that is to hire some hungry earthquake to come along and gobble up Kansas.[1]

But Kansas has also been backward in projects dear to the heart of progressive citizens. The state government has never adopted the initiative and referendum system; it has never used its recall powers in the case of any state officer; and it has never held a convention to rewrite its ninety-year-old constitution, although that document has been amended so many times its authors would hardly recognize it now. To date, 61 amendments have been proposed since the Wyandotte Constitution was written. Of these, 39 amendments have been adopted.

On the other hand, Kansas was among the first states to adopt the primary election system and abrogate state conven-

[1] *Emporia Gazette*, April 25, 1922.

tions, where deals—and misdeals—were made in "smoke-filled hotel rooms." Kansas was the seventh state to adopt suffrage for women, the other six states being west of Kansas. Similarly, Kansas established a system whereby United States senators were nominated and elected by direct vote, long before Congress provided for direct elections. And, as an aid to better legislation, Kansas was the first state to organize a successful legislative council to study and furnish information about proposed legislation. Several other states had organized such councils, but Kansas was the first to supplement the council with a research bureau designed to unearth information. When a project of statewide interest comes up, the council, composed of ten senators and fifteen representatives, begins a continuing study of the proposal. At each meeting the research bureau submits a report on the facts it has gathered. The bureau may query other states, or even foreign countries, about what has been done in similar circumstances and then present this information to the council. The result is that little ineffective legislation passes through the lawmaking body, as was the case when unstudied bills were presented.

Kansas was also one of the first states to adopt a ballot on which the name of the candidate, not the party which sponsors him, is prominently displayed. It was among the first to prohibit secret societies as political parties. And it early established a literacy test to prevent the illiterate and the easily swayed foreign-born from voting in elections. The law provided that no able-bodied man or woman without physical or mental handicaps could have help in marking a ballot. By this law the state was able to head off the development of political machines in many of the larger cities.

Dr. S. J. Crumbine, for many years secretary of the State Board of Health, has written of the early progress in public health in Kansas.[2] Dr. Crumbine put Kansas on the map, so far as pure foods and drugs and honest weights are concerned.

[2] *Frontier Doctor* (Philadelphia, Dorrance and Company, 1948).

The Panorama of the Bluestem Hills

Not only did he discover scales which cheated both the grocer and the customer, but he also gathered up a bushel basket of metal, nails, and wire used by druggists in their prescription scales. One-third of the prescriptions written in the state during one month were incorrectly compounded because of weighted scales. In the course of another investigation, Dr. Crumbine borrowed three dogs of about equal size and weight and fed them the same food for a month, except that the hamburger fed to one dog contained no preservatives, while that fed to the other two contained two different preservatives generally used by meat dealers and packers. At the end of the month the dog that had been fed pure food had gained in weight and health, while the other two had deteriorated in both respects. The Board of Health then presented to the packers and dealers a prohibition against the use of either preservative.

Dr. Crumbine once picked up a common drinking glass on a railroad train, scraped off the film around the edge, and had the residue analyzed. The analysis showed the glass heavily laden with tuberculosis germs. He gathered up glasses on other trains, and soon along came an order from the board banning common drinking cups from all public buildings, trains, and soda fountains. Outraged railroad officials and businessmen protested at such arbitrary laws, and some even went to court. But the orders remained in force. Dr. Crumbine was also responsible for the banning of roller towels in public washrooms, after it was discovered that syphilis germs might be transmitted by them.

For some time the doctor had been certain that the common house fly was the carrier of many diseases, but he had found no successful method of getting rid of them. He attended a baseball game one day, and during an exciting inning a voice boomed from the bleachers, "Swat a fly!" Dr. Crumbine came home from the game with an idea for a sweeping campaign, with "Swat the Fly" as its slogan. Mayors issued "Swat the Fly" proclamations; women's clubs promoted clean-up drives; and merchants offered prizes to boys and girls bringing in the largest number of house flies, "dead or alive." The movement spread, and "Swat the Fly" soon became a slogan throughout the country. Along with the drive went a campaign to prohibit the transport of fresh meats without flyproof covering.

Another early ruling was made on the use of the word "cure" as part of the name of several patent medicines. While the medicines might be helpful in preventing or alleviating diseases, they certainly were not cures, and the Board of Health drove them out of the state until the labels and advertising were altered.

When Dr. Crumbine and his epidemiologist decided to disprove the theory that a stream purified itself every seven miles of flow, the two rented a boat and floated fifty miles down the Kaw River from Topeka to Lawrence. They took samples of the water every quarter-mile and delivered them to chemists at Lawrence. The samples showed that water half-way downriver contained just as much sewage contamination as that within two miles of the Topeka sewer outlets and that at no point was the contamination reduced as much as 30 per cent. The result was a law requiring every city in Kansas to treat all sewage before dumping it into any stream.

These are only a few of the accomplishments of Dr. Crumbine, a man to whom Kansans owe much of their present health and well-being.

The earliest settlers brought their churches and church schools with them. The first baptism in present Kansas was probably performed by Father Padilla in 1541, when he accompanied Coronado to the region. The first church established for white settlers was the Plymouth Congregational Church at Lawrence. The first Sunday school was established by the Methodists in April, 1855, at a home in Brownsville (now Auburn, Shawnee County). There were ten scholars in the school, and Sam Cavender was the first superintendent.

It may be, of course, that Fort Leavenworth and Fort Riley had chapels where regular religious services were held. Indian missions were established by the Methodists, the Presbyterians, the Quakers, and the Catholics twenty years or more before Kansas was opened to settlement. But the first church and the first church school established after the arrival of the first settlers were those at Lawrence and Auburn.

The Kansas bank deposit guaranty law was one of the earliest in the country and was the forerunner of the present federal deposit insurance system, though the Kansas law had been abrogated years before the federal system was set in operation. The difficulty with the Kansas system was that surplus was limited, and the many failures during the depression after World War I made it impossible to pay more than a part of the losses. The bankers for the most part hated the law, and when it became known that losses would be heavy, there were no more assessments, and bank depositors were left holding the bag for more than two million dollars.

Another reform of the same period was the Blue Sky Law, which antedated the Securities and Exchange Commission by some thirty years. The Kansas law was designed to stop the exploitation of inexperienced businessmen and widows left with property. The law required an examination of all prospective stock and bond projects and the licensing of all salesmen. There was a great protest by swindlers who had been prospering at the expense of widows and orphans and by bankers who had been selling worthless securities they had taken in as collateral. But despite opposition the laws were held valid, and by the time the federal government began to offer protection to the public many states had already followed Kansas' lead.

2 2: *The Grass Grows Green*

KANSAS, like Caesar's Gaul, is divided into three parts. The grasses which flourish so abundantly throughout the state mark the three areas distinctly. In flying across the state from east to west, one may note the difference in almost any season. The grass grows green in Kansas, but some grows greener.

In the east may be found the lovely and succulent bluegrass, which has largely supplanted the native grasses. Then come the Blue Stem Hills, on which grows the distinctive grass that gives this part of the state the reputation as the most extensive and efficient cattle-fattening area in the country. The bluestem grasses extend west of the hills, deep into the high plains area.

As one reaches the high plains, roughly the western half of the state, the bluestem surrenders its predominance to the short grass, or buffalo grass. The belts in which the grasses flourish seemingly follow certain rainfall patterns, the short grass taking over as moisture diminishes.

Even the introduction of other grasses has failed to change this botanic partition. Alfalfa does well throughout the state, and the deep green of the tame hay decorates the valley lands far into Colorado. In fact, at the turn of the century Kansas was the nation's largest producer of this crop and is still one of the major growing areas.

Of the three dominant pasture grasses, two are native to the state. In preterritorial days the eastern part of the state was covered with several wild prairie grasses, including large areas of native bluestem. The Reverend Thomas Johnson, a Methodist missionary to the Shawnee Indians and founder of the famous Shawnee manual labor school near Kansas City, is credited with bringing Kentucky bluegrass to Kansas and establishing it as the predominant pasture and lawn grass of the eastern hills.

Johnson brought the grass seed from Kentucky, and as he traveled on horseback across the territory he scattered the grass seed from his saddlebags. Kentucky bluegrass is the first grass to be seen in the spring as the snow and ice melt and, except for a brief dormant period during the hot days of July and August, it provides a verdent carpet until early winter. Besides providing pasture, this plant produces large quantities of seed, which is an important cash crop on many farms. At one time, before the pure seed laws were enacted, Kansas actually produced more Kentucky bluegrass seed for commercial purposes than did Kentucky itself. The seed produced now is still the Kentucky bluegrass, though "Kentucky" has been dropped from the name.

The cleft between the bluegrass and the bluestem regions is marked geographically as well as botanically. An abrupt uplift of limestone forms what Kansans now call the Blue Stem Hills, which start near the Nebraska line and extend without a break into Oklahoma. At the eastern edge of these hills begins the bluestem grass. So pronounced is the difference in vista that the traveler who might miss the change in color cannot fail to note the change in landscape.

The Blue Stem Hills comprise about four million acres in Kansas, the belt varying in width from thirty to sixty miles as it girds the state. Many of the early settlers regarded the hills, then called the Flint Hills, as wasteland and took claims only in the valleys. It was not until twenty years after statehood that cattlemen properly appraised the value of the area. Then for a time they exploited the grasses almost to the point of extinction.

Even the years of drought failed to destroy the Kansas bluestem. During the arid thirties, much of the pastureland was too dry to support any kind of crop. But given measurable moisture, the grasses seem to leap from the earth and attain record heights.

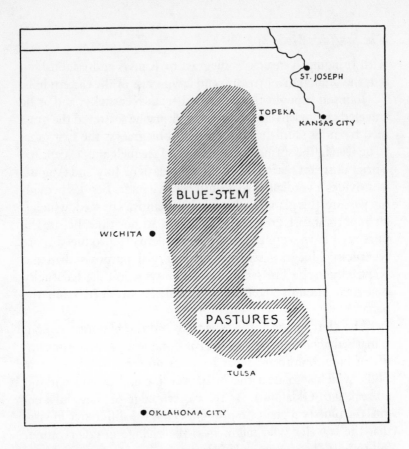

About 400,000 range cattle are brought into the Blue Stem Hills every April for fattening. Most of these are steers from ranges in Texas and New Mexico; others come from Colorado and Wyoming. The reason is apparent: here is the largest area in the United States where a steer can be fattened three to four pounds a day throughout the spring and summer. There are bluestem grasses all over the central states, from Texas to Quebec between the Appalachians and the Rockies, but nowhere else is the area so vast or the grass so productive. This efficiency is said to be caused by the limestone content of the soil. The topsoil is so thin that the grass roots readily tap the lime and absorb it. The process is described by H. R. Hilton as follows:

The tough and heavy sod of the Blue Stem pastures attest that they are the survival of the fittest. Neither alfalfa or red clover or blue grass, or any other legume or cultivated grass can excell the native blue stem in putting on flesh and in increasing the weight of beef steers during the summer pasturing season.

There are at least five ledges of limestone between the levels of the valleys and the highest plateaus, and where each ledge out-crops, there is a line of broken lime rock of various thicknesses in the process of weathering. This weathered material is being spread over all the slopes below each outcrop by every shower of rain and through the agency of these passing showers, the supply of lime at the grass roots is being constantly renewed and maintained at the maximum. Lime rock and blue stem pastures are the out-standing characteristics of this "grassy quadrangle" the largest block of almost continuous richly sodded pasture land in the United States devoted almost exclusively to the feeding and breeding of cattle. The lime rock is the vitalizer and stimulator of every plant that grows in the soil within this quadrangle.[1]

Two varieties of bluestem predominate in this region. The "big bluestem" grows primarily in the valleys and is characteristically much larger and coarser than the "little blue stem." In rainy years big bluestem will grow stalks taller than a man. It has been noted that in an especially productive season a man on horseback can almost be hidden by the grass.

The little bluestem resists drought much more effectively than its brother. It is to be found on the sides and tops of the hills and has often been referred to as bunch grass because it tends to grow in clumps. Both varieties mature and cure in the pasture, and both make excellent prairie hay when cut at the proper time.

William Allen White described the bluestem pastures as he saw them at his home in Emporia, on the eastern edge of the hills:

[1] *Quarterlies* of the Kansas State Board of Agriculture, Twenty-sixth Biennial Report (1928).

We shall not have much wheat in this part of Kansas. It was too wet to sow in the fall. It looks like a corn year, but a corn crop is six months off with drouth, chinch bugs, frost and high winds lurking in the future's utmost rim. But one crop, we in this part of Kansas are just dead sure of—the blue stem grass. It is, after all, the most important crop in the kingdom of the big red steer. The blue stem is soaked at the roots.

The blue stem is not subject to bugs. The blue stem, even in drouth, does not wither until August. The pasture ponds are full. The creeks are all chuckling under the ice. The ground of the upland and of the second bottoms has been water soaked all winter. Walk across the pastures and you can see a green shadow staining the earth around you. Salute the great crop, the profitable crop![2]

W. J. Tod, operator of one of the most extensive fine-cattle breeding and fattening projects at Maple Hill and in Texas and New Mexico, spoke from long experience about the bluestem grasses when he said:

Kansas grass is one of the most important crops—perhaps THE most important crop—in the state. When you consider that we have still over 14½ million acres of native grass and nearly a million acres of other grasses, and that the Kansas native grass for at least a third of the year, cannot be excelled, if equalled, as a beef producer, we may realize what a wonderful asset we have in our grass lands. These millions of acres of grass capable of producing in the summer months alone, say fifty pounds of beef per acre, and during the winter months affording roughage for the vast herds we carry over, show what a splendid inheritance we have in our grazing lands.[3]

Mr. Tod was so impressed with the tremendous value of the bluestem pastures that he directed in his will:

It is furthermore my special wish and request that care should be taken to preserve the natural prairie grasses and that none of the prairie grasslands should be plowed or broken up during the

[2] *Emporia Gazette* (date unknown).
[3] From an address quoted in *Report* of Kansas State Board of Agriculture, Vol. XLV, No. 177 (March, 1926), 9.

lifetime of my wife, Margaret, and that great care shall be taken to avoid their being overstocked at any time.[4]

It should not be surprising that the early settlers and visitors to western Kansas came away with a rather poor opinion of its potentialities. These visitors came from the East, where the hills were covered with timber and the grass grew lush in the lowlands and the uplands, where the rains came regularly and in good quantity and the snowfall was heavy and prolonged. From that area they came into rolling prairie country, where from the top of nearly any hill was an almost limitless view of the indigenous short grass, which grew nowhere else in the world.

Along the creeks one might see cottonwood trees bearing evidence of a long life. But the trees were small and generally few in number. At many places along the old trails one could see for twenty-five to thirty miles in any direction across treeless plains.

The wind blew unceasingly across the high prairies, where it might restrain itself to a gentle breeze or release a storm of tornadic proportions, whipping sand and dust into one's face and cutting the skin. Even the hardy mules and horses of the stagecoach outfits turned their heads away from such winds.

Pike, Long, and Greeley agreed that the high plains area was not a goodly clime. They did not believe, or perhaps had not read, Coronado's declaration that the soil was the richest he had ever seen. The early visitors to Kansas saw only the landscape, not its elements. They could not know that the short grass country was destined to play an important role in feeding the world through two world wars and that it would produce the largest crop of hard winter wheat in the entire world. Nor could they visualize that the buffalo grass would have great value. True, they saw the buffalo and the antelope wax fat and sleek on it and the prairie dogs grow roly-poly from

[4] *Quarterlies* of the Kansas State Board of Agriculture, Twenty-seventh Biennial Report (1930), 313.

eating its roots. To C. K. Holliday may be given a good deal of the credit for realizing the real worth of the short grass country. Holliday has earlier been described as a Pennsylvanian who helped found the city of Topeka and promoted the Atchison, Topeka and Santa Fé Railroad. He proposed that his railroad be built across the prairies to the mountains, and along the mountains to Santa Fé, New Mexico, the starting point of the Santa Fé Trail.

The trail drivers and passengers on the stagecoaches told of seeing vast herds of buffalo grazing on the short grasses. Often the wagon trains would pass for days through herds extending as far as the eye could see. Men would count animals by the hour and then estimate the number in a single herd. Their estimates varied from ten to fifteen million animals. Government men calculated that the total in two great herds was somewhere between seventeen and twenty million head.

When Holliday went to New York and Boston to raise the money for his railroad, financiers objected to building a railroad through uninhabited and, they believed, uninhabitable regions. Holliday would reply that a country which could support ten to fifteen million buffalo could support an equal or greater number of domestic cattle and sheep. Soil must be rich that could feed vast herds throughout the year, and that soil would grow wheat, corn, and other eastern crops, and perhaps crops as yet unknown. The roar of the buffalo bulls would be replaced by the lowing of domestic cattle and sheep, and the wail of the coyote would be replaced by the baying of dogs at the moon.

How right Holliday was took years to prove, but he lived to see his prophesy come true. His prediction about new crops also came true with the introduction of alfalfa and the various sorghums which now play so important a part in the farm operations of western Kansas.

About one-third of the state remains virgin prairie today. The Blue Stem Hills and vast expanses of land in western Kansas are unsuitable for cultivation and are covered with grass.

A considerable portion of the high plains area which was broken during World War I when wheat crops were vital has since been returned to buffalo grass. The state agricultural experiment station at Hays has developed a seed-harvesting machine which gathers buffalo grass seed to aid in restoring potential dust-bowl regions to grazing lands.

Buffalo grass has one unusual characteristic in that it cures on the ground and retains its nutritional qualities throughout the winter months. Livestock subsists on the grass equally well in the winter and the summer. Further, the buffalo grass does not grow in bunches or clumps but lies rather flat on the ground. Since the winter snows generally blow off the grass into ravines, the grass provides ready year-round pasturage.

Buffalo grass does not have the dark green appearance of bluegrass, bluestem, and other native grasses of the midwest and eastern regions. Even in the best years—that is, years of plentiful rainfall—the buffalo grass is a light green color. When it matures it becomes even lighter and in the fall and winter presents a very pale, almost whitish-green appearance. It contrasts sharply with alfalfa and the grama grasses and in winter contrasts even more sharply with the dark green winter wheat.

The value of buffalo grass is well recognized among stockmen, and in recent years there has been considerable development of pasture management throughout the western part of Kansas. Many hundreds of acres of marginal wheat land have been taken out of cultivation and restored to buffalo grass range to save the soil from wind and water erosion and provide more pasture for livestock.

So important are the grasses to the livelihood of Kansas that active efforts have been made to bring that importance to the attention of the nation. It is not sufficient that workers in the livestock industry alone should appreciate these bounties.

J. C. Mohler, for thirty-five years secretary of the Kansas Board of Agriculture, long advocated that Kansas build a monument to its grasses and suggested that a park be established in the Blue Stem Hills. The Kansas Chamber of Commerce examined the idea and suggested merely a highway through the hills. Mohler did not follow that line of reasoning. He wrote:

To properly see and fully appreciate the hills and the marvelous views one must leave the highway and get far back in the vast expanse of the hills. There one finds vistas of utter loveliness. But they are practically inaccessible to the public. So we ought to have a park so that people may easily reach vantage points and freely enjoy what must be one of God's masterpieces.

The fascination of the Blue Stem Hills lies not only in their rugged, broken terrain, but in the overwhelming opulence of a fertile land that stretches to the far horizons. Grass, grass, oceans of grass, with lone elms and clustered trees dotting the varied landscape and a profusion of wild flowers that lend color to enchantment. Back in the recesses of the hills, where no signs of habitation are visible, one feels far removed from the dross of civilization and may find that peace that passeth understanding, while from the summit of a majestic height there is unfolded a panorama of indescribable beauty, the regal expanse of luxuriant blue stem, tree fringed streams, of valleys checkered with crops, imposing ranch headquarters of enduring native stone, and distant villages that nestle among the hills as though they were a part and parcel of nature's artistry.

As Mohler pointed out when he started his campaign, "No one can get the real feel or see the beauties of the hills unless he gets a horse or a mule or just takes a walk for a mile or two away from the highways and wanders around in places that no motor car could ever navigate."

There are now five highways cutting through the Blue Stem Hills from east to west. These highways present about as satisfactory a view of the wide sweep of the hills as could be provided. For the most part, they are the work of engineers concerned with easy grades and convenient traveling conditions. Motorists can go racing over the hills with utter disregard for the beauty of the region. Certainly, these hills are lovely monuments to our grasses at any time of the year tourists might choose for traveling. The sharp escarpments, high bluffs, and narrow valleys covered with the changing colors of the seasons and the endless vistas of rolling prairies spotted with great herds of cattle could become a national park of greater meaning to Americans than many now in existence.

Apart from their aesthetic value, the hills inspire other comment. As Rolla Clymer wrote in the *El Dorado Times*:

By their own majesty the hills reveal the puny stature of man and the futility of his own exertions. If it's peace and quiet you want, Mister Man, that dispensation is right at your door and may be had for a trifling effort. You may receive it in large portions or small, depending upon your desire and need.

John J. Ingalls is regarded by many as the most erudite writer the state has ever produced. One of the classic essays he penned was the one on grass, excerpts of which follow:

Next in importance to the divine profusion of water, light and air, those three great physical facts which render existence possible, may be reckoned the beneficence of grass. Exaggerated by tropical heats and vapors to the gigantic cane congested with its saccharine secretion, or dwarfed by polar rigors to the fibrous hair of northern solitudes, embracing between these extremes the maize with its resolute pennons, the rice plant of southern swamps, the wheat, rye, barley, oats, and other cereals, no less than the humbler verdure of hillside, pasture and prairie in the temperate zone, grass is the most widely distributed of all vegetable beings, and is at once the type of our life and the emblem of our mortality.

As he reflected upon the brevity of human life, grass has been the favorite symbol of the moralist, the chosen theme of the philosopher. "All flesh is grass," said the prophet; "My days are as the grass," sighed the troubled patriarch; and the pensive Nebuchadnezzar, in his penitential mood, exceeded even these, and, as the sacred historian informs us, "did eat grass like an ox."

Lying in the sunshine among the buttercups and the dandelions of May, scarcely higher in intelligence than the minute tenants of that mimic wilderness, our earliest recollections are of grass; and when the fitful fever is ended and the foolish wrangle of the market and the forum is closed, grass heals over the scar which our descent into the bosom of the earth has made, and the carpet of the infant becomes the blanket of the dead.

Grass is the forgiveness of Nature—her constant benediction. Fields trampled with battle, saturated with blood, torn with the ruts of cannon, grow green again with grass, and carnage is forgotten.

Streets abandoned by traffic becomes grass-grown like rural lanes and are obliterated. Forests decay, harvests perish, flowers vanish, but grass is immortal. Beleagured by the sullen hosts of winter, it withdraws into the impregnable fortress of its subterranean vitality and emerges upon the first solicitation of spring. Sown by the winds, by the wandering birds, propagated by the subtle agriculture of the elements, which are its ministers and its servants, it softens the rude outline of the world.

It bears no blazonry of blooms to charm the senses with its fragrance or splendor, but its homely hue is more enchanting than the lily or the rose. It yields no fruit in earth or air, and yet, should its harvest fail for a single year, famine would depopulate the world.[5]

For all these reasons, it can be said with justification that the Blue Stem Hills represent Kansas to the nation.

[5] "Blue Grass," *Kansas Magazine*, Vol. I (1872).

2 3: *The Kansas Vista*

O NE FEATURE of the Kansas scene has been sadly neglected. It appears that many tourists and visitors have
never been told about the unusual scenery to be
found in the Sunflower State. A number of persons,
including some Kansans, regard the state only as a land of rolling prairies and great expanses of wheat, corn, and sorghum.
Many even believe that the western half of the state is flat.

There are many scenic areas in the state which offer a
matchless variety of natural and man-made beauties. Some of
the more spectacular are to be found in the western section,
where the buffalo once roamed, the prairie dog had his habitat,
and the short grass grew unrestrained. The scene varies from
the lovely sylvan areas of the eastern third of the state and the
ancient Indian burial grounds in central Kansas to the ruins of
an ancient Indian pueblo in the far west. There are dozens of
gleaming lakes, some of which present a veritable fairyland,
and there are natural wonders to excite the praise of the most
blasé traveler.

Kansas may be said to be unique in that one may see virgin
areas adjoining cultivated and productive farms, while only a
short distance away a highly industrialized community carries
on the complex affairs of business. In this respect Kansas offers
an open window through which America, past and present,
can be seen in all its glory.

From the high bluffs in the northeast to the high plains in
the southwest, the state is rich in color, atmosphere, and history. Kansas may justly be accused of neglect in failing to provide adequate highways to many of the unusual and bizarre
scenic wonders. Since few of the sights border the main highways, tourists rarely obtain more than a superficial knowledge

of the state. Some of these wonders are so difficult to reach that even native Kansans are unaware of their existence.

The state geological survey has published an illustrated booklet[1] about the geological formations to be found in Kansas, a number of which could compete with the nation's well-publicized, and therefore famous, wonders. The booklet tells the location of each formation, discusses its causes, and gives precise directions on how to reach it.

Evidence of the glaciers that once covered parts of the state may be seen at many points in northeastern Kansas, where the terrific pressure of the ice cut through the hills and caused great upheavals. Glacial moraines and other marks of the ice age are found south of the Kaw River, and the many boulders bear witness to the relentless movement of the ice. The church facing the east wing of the Kansas Statehouse in Topeka is constructed of glacial boulders, and many homes, fireplaces, and fences also have been built of these granite or conglomerate formations. Boulders have been found that are too large to be moved by modern machinery. Others have never been excavated, and their exact size cannot be determined.

At Rock City in central Kansas one can see more than two hundred concretions formed by the work of underground water on native sandstone. As Kenneth K. Landes of the geological survey wrote, "Some are almost perfect spheres with diameters exceeding twelve feet. Others, with diameters from 8 to 27 feet, vary from rounded to elliptical forms. At one time, when the surface of the land in this area was higher than it is now, the sandstone rock occupying this space consisted of poorly cemented sand grains. Underground waters containing dissolved calcium carbonate circulated through these porous rocks, depositing calcium carbonate in the open spaces. The precipitation of this calcium carbonate, which is natural cement, began at many scattered points and continued outward

[1] Kenneth Landes, "Scenic Kansas," University of Kansas, State Geological Survey of Kansas (December 1, 1935).

A Stone Fence Post

in all directions from these centers. In this matter spherical bodies of tightly cemented sand grains—concretions—were formed within the sandstone mass. As erosion by wind, rain and running water lowered the surface, carrying away the loosely cemented sand, the concretions were uncovered."

There are also many sinkholes, caves, and tunnels carved by water as it coursed through soft rock, sandstone, limestone, and gypsum. "Hell's Half Acre," a name given to the ten acres of colorful and bizarre formations in Comanche County, resembles somewhat the Bad Lands of South Dakota. There are many pulpit rocks in the area, which were cut by rain wash, running water, and wind. Occasionally, a canyon entrance or exit has been cut through the rocks, and the white sandstone, with its brown and yellow bands, and the vivid red of the canyon provide a sharp contrast to the green of the trees growing in the canyon.

St. Jacob's Well, in Barber County, is the oldest of the sinkholes, as indicated by the number of large trees growing around its edge. Such sinks are caused by the solutional work of subsurface waters. The water dissolves and carries away the soluble rock, then the roof caves in to create large holes, which are often asserted to be bottomless. Some of these have formed within recent years.

Kansas has many natural bridges. The one near Sun City, also in Barber County, is 50 feet long and 35 feet wide and has approximately 12 feet of clearance over the stream bed. Near the bridge is a tunnel about 250 feet long, formed in somewhat the same manner.

Millions of years ago, in the Cretaceous Period, much of western Kansas was covered by a great inland sea. The lands bordering the sea were low and swampy, and the streams were sluggish. Millions of shellfish lived in the waters, and the shells accumulated on the sea floor, thus creating the chalk beds of Kansas, which are famous throughout the world for the variety and sizes of fossils found in them. About 800 feet of chalk and chalky shales were deposited in the ancient sea. When the winds and the rain carried away the surface rocks, the chalk beds were exposed. Many of the animals living in this region were very large—fossils 50 feet long and turtle shells 11 feet across have been excavated, as well as fossils of birds with teeth and with wingspreads of 26 feet.

Wind and water erosion has molded some of the chalk beds into fantastic shapes. Pinnacles, small buttes, and spires have been formed which suggest such names as "mushroom rocks," "the sphynx," and "monument rocks." The great Cedar Bluff Reservoir on the Smoky Hill River is situated on chalk cliffs.

There is a small area in Ellsworth County containing unusual formations of flaming-red rock. The colorful and oddly shaped rocks may best be seen in Red Rock Canyon.

Another natural phenomenon to be found in western Kansas is the disappearing river, known as the Whitewoman River, which rises in Colorado, crosses into Kansas, and goes underground in the third tier of counties. The maps show the point where the stream disappears, to flow on underground toward the Arkansas River.

The Whitewoman River creates what was long known as the "Shallow Water Empire," north of Garden City. Much of the wide and level valley constituting the Shallow Water is irrigated by pumping and is one of the important potato and alfalfa regions of the state.

In southeastern Kansas man has created scenery that is rarely found in other parts of the country. The ravages of strip coal-mining operations, the ridges and lakes formed as giant electric shovels removed the covering of earth and rocks from shallow layers of minerals, have resulted in a unique vista. Many of the barren piles have been transformed by nature into timberland, and man in turn has stepped in to create parks and recreation areas of unusual beauty.

Lovely scenery is also to be found in the twenty-odd state parks and in countless county and city parks that have been created around artificial lakes. Kansas is not endowed with natural bodies of water, but the terrain is such that the riverways may be dammed to create areas of rugged or sylvan beauty, as taste demands.

In recent years Kansas has become increasingly aware of what it has to offer to satisfy man's longing for the beautiful and the unusual. The natural and man-made attractions are of a distinctive quality that should compel tourists to visit the state.

24: *Salt*

KANSAS has long been one of the major producers of salt, and in recent years it has ranked sixth in tonnage and fifth in the value of salt produced throughout the United States.

Some years ago the Kansas Geological Survey calculated that there was salt beneath at least 7,500 square miles of the state's area. The strata varied in thickness from a few feet to as much as 400 to 1,000 feet, and it was estimated that the total salt deposit was about five trillion tons.

That figure was so astronomical that the geologists made further calculations and produced the statement that if the entire salt deposit were raised to the surface it would cover the entire area of the state (nearly 82,000 square miles) to a depth of 37 feet. It was further estimated that if the salt supply of central Kansas were built into a solid prism 5 miles square, the prism would reach to a height of 23 miles—about four times higher than Mount Everest, the highest known mountain in the world. Further, the geologists stated that the total salt deposit in Kansas, if raised to the surface, would build a wall 2 miles wide and 1,000 feet high around the state—some 1,300 miles. Kenneth L. Landes, of the geological survey, concluded that Kansas had enough salt to supply all the needs of the country for over a half million years.

The salt deposits in present Kansas were known to the Indians long before white men visited the region. In their explorations of the area early in the nineteenth century, Lieutenant Zebulon Pike and Major Stephen H. Long noted the many salt springs and marshes in Central Kansas, where the salt deposits either were near the surface or were brought to the surface by water erosion. There are twelve salt creeks in the state, all of them somewhat brackish at times. The Saline River was given its name by early explorers and settlers, who found the creek salty at low-water periods.

Kansas could have enjoyed an important monopoly in salt production if it had followed up a project begun in territorial days. In the ordinance of 1861 the Wyandotte Constitutional Convention incorporated a provision which directed that twelve salt springs and six sections of land surrounding each spring were to be allotted to the state for its exclusive use. The allotment was made, and the state land commission, named by Charles Robinson, the first governor of the state, selected the springs and the surrounding lands, but the state never carried out the project. Later, the springs and the 72 sections of land were conveyed to the first state normal school (now Emporia State Teachers College) as an endowment.

The twelve salt springs chosen by the Kansas land commissioners were:

No. 1, in Ottawa County
No. 2, in Mitchell County
No. 3, in Mitchell County
No. 4, in Saline County
No. 5, in Saline County
No. 6, in Mitchell County
No. 7, in Republic County
No. 8, in Republic County

No. 9, in Republic County[1]
No. 10, in Cloud County
No. 11, in Cloud County
No. 12, in Cloud County

In 1863 the legislature passed an act which was designed to encourage the production of salt and authorized the leasing of the state-owned salt springs to those who would agree to manufacture salt from the saline waters for sale to the residents of the state. Each lease provided that the holders should produce not less than five hundred barrels of salt per year, or the lease might be forfeited. Only one of the leases was ever canceled for failure to meet the production requirements. The leases were made to four separate groups of men, who promised to operate the equipment. (At that time salt was produced by the evaporation process.) The legislature thus provided a bounty to the salt producers, in that it made no charge for the leases or for the salt, in consideration for the actual production of a specified amount of salt from each of the springs.

The first official geological report on the salt deposits in Kansas was published in 1866 by the first state geologist, B. F. Mudge:

> The great supply of salt, which is to meet the demands of Kansas and neighboring states, lies at various depths in a tract of country about thirty-five miles wide and eighty miles long, crossing the Republican, Solomon and Saline valleys. The signs of the deposits are seen in numerous springs, but more frequently in extensive salt marshes.

Professor Mudge found that 69 gallons of brine from the state-owned salt spring in Republic County would produce a bushel of salt containing only 2½ per cent impurities. It was concluded that the brine came from a great bed only slightly contaminated by limestone and soil.

[1] The adjacent lands were claimed by Republic, Cloud, and Jewell counties.

While a large number of the salt deposits in Kansas contain pure salt, there are also strata which contain impurities. In some areas the top stratum may be composed of 35 feet of salt and shale, with the stratum beneath composed of 20 feet of almost pure salt. The strata of salt and shale vary in thickness from 5 to 50 feet, while the salt deposits may be over 300 feet thick.

It has been estimated by geologists that eighty feet of sea water must evaporate to make one foot of salt. There was, of course, a wide range in the amount of salt water precipitated at various times, and there may have been intervening floods which resulted in heavy layers of mud that later consolidated into shale. It may be of interest to check the drilling log of a typical well drilled in the Hutchinson area. The well went down through nearly five hundred feet of sand, soft stone, and limestone, at which point the top of the salt stratum was reached. Here are the log records:

Salt and shale	33 feet
Salt	20
Salt and shale	15
Salt	10
Salt and shale	10
Salt	15
Salt and shale	5
Salt	20
Salt and shale	5
Salt	5
Salt and shale	5
Salt	15
Salt and shale	10
Salt	30
Salt and shale	15
Salt	15
Salt and shale	20
Salt	50
Salt and shale	15
Salt	15
Total	328

Salt has long played an important part in history, religion, and superstition. History records that early German tribes fought for many years for the possession of salt springs. Since salt was believed to come directly from the gods, those who lived near salt deposits had great powers of intercession, and their lands were much coveted.

There are many biblical references to salt; everyone remembers the fate of Lot's wife. In the early days covenants were sealed with salt, and Numbers 18:19 makes a direct reference to the "covenant of salt." The Persians believed salt to be an emblem of purity, and a traitor was said to be "untrue to salt." Incidentally, the accepted picture of the Last Supper shows a saltcellar overturned in front of Judas Iscariot.

Many historians believe that the earliest trade routes were formed for trade in salt. One of the oldest highways in Italy, the Via Salaria or "salt highway," was used to carry salt from the fields at Ostia to the Sabine Hills. When the Romans conquered England, they found a series of highways radiating from salt wells. These roads were known as the "upper" or "lower" saltways.

In ancient times nations placed a high tax on salt. The tax was graduated on the basis of the purity of the salt, and consequently only "dirty" or contaminated salt was available to the poor. Cakes of salt were used as money in Abyssinia, parts of Africa, and many other countries of the ancient world. A bag of salt still serves as barter among the tribes of central Africa who are not able to reach salt deposits because of hostile neighbors. It is recorded that slave traders often carried large supplies of salt to Africa to be traded for slaves.

It is interesting to note that the word salary comes directly from the Latin *sal*, meaning "salt." In the days of the Roman Empire soldiers and their officers were payed, in addition to their wages, a *salarium*, or allowance for salt. Before and after this time the soldiers were given a regular supply of salt.

For centuries the mineral has been used in religious rites, and even today in some countries babies are sprinkled with salt, which is supposed to give them strength, vigor, and longevity. In other countries expectant mothers sprinkle salt on the roofs of their homes so that witches who might come to cast a spell on the baby will be too busy picking up the salt grains to disturb the infant.

While salt is one of the cheapest minerals, it was once sold in Kansas for its weight in gold. When Colonel Sumner and his troops came into the territory in 1857, the horses and the men were so starved for salt that a settler in Rice County sold it to them at the rate of one five-dollar gold piece a spoonful.

During the early days in Kansas, frugal settlers bought land containing salt springs and evaporated the brine in crude utensils. Often they would set a pan or keg of brine in the sun to evaporate and then scrape the salt crystals off the sides and bottom of the vessel. They also sold brine to their neighbors, who evaporated it by the same process and sold the salt to travelers. But most of the pioneers to eastern Kansas brought salt with them from Michigan and New York—an expensive practice which soon led the founding fathers of the state to take steps to protect the natural supply of salt.

For many years, J. G. Tuthill was believed to have been the first commercial producer of salt in Kansas. He had claimed land in Republic County which contained salt marshes. But in 1945 Robert Taft of the University of Kansas, in a paper presented to the Kansas Academy of Science, presented evidence that commercial production first began at Osawatomie, where the Osawatomie Salt Works, owned by William Chesnut and others, produced salt by evaporation as early as 1863. The brine was obtained from five wells which had originally been drilled in search of oil. At one time the salt works had 17 thirty-gallon kettles. The salt produced at Osawatomie sold for $1.40 a bushel of 56 pounds.

To encourage the production of salt, in 1863 the state enacted a law offering a bounty of ten cents a bushel up to ten thousands bushels annually. So far as the records disclose, no one ever applied to collect the bounty.

In 1866, a writer in the *New York Tribune* described the vast possibilities in salt production in Kansas. Soon after, a group of men from New Bedford, Massachusetts, came to the state and drilled a six-hundred-foot well near Solomon City. The company had thirty evaporation vats and produced many bushels of salt in 1869, possibly the first large-scale production. The company changed hands about 1881, when the plant was enlarged to produce about ten thousand barrels of salt a year. The plant continued in operation until after 1898.

About 1887, commercial development of the salt deposits became a major industry in Kansas. Evaporation plants were set up at many points, from Sumner and Harper counties on the southern border to Republic County on the northern border. For many years there was a solar reduction plant at Solomon, which shipped salt over the old Kansas Pacific Railway to eastern points.

Ben Blanchard discovered the great salt bed underlying Reno County in 1887, which a New York firm, Goinlock and Humphrey, exploited for a time. Within a year after this discovery thirteen plants had opened in Reno County, producing a total of some nine million barrels of salt annually. Salt mining began at about the same time, and there is rock-salt production at Lyons, Hutchinson, and Kanopolis at the present time.

Only a comparatively small amount of the salt produced in Kansas, or as a matter of fact, that produced in the other major salt-producing states, ever flows through the salt shakers of American homes. The largest amounts go to the manufacturers of soda ash and caustic soda, the two most common sodium compounds. A considerable amount of salt is used as glazing for ceramics, tiles, pottery, and other clay and shale products. The packers use a large amount in the preparation and preserving of meats, and ice-cream manufacturers also require large quantities of salt for freezing their products. Livestock producers and feeders buy large amounts of cubed salt.

The yearly salt production in Kansas runs to approximately one million tons and is valued at about four million dollars—a truly vital industry, both to the state and to the nation.

25: *A Producer of Sweetness*

KANSAS may never have flowed with milk and honey, but at one time, even before the days of the beet-sugar industry around Garden City, Kansas was a producer of sugar. The sugar produced in Kansas would not be popular with housewives of today, though the crop from which the sugar was extracted still grows abundantly on Kansas farms.

There are many citizens who can remember when sweet sorghums were grown for the making of blackstrap molasses, or "long sweetenin'," an important staple in the diet of people throughout the southern and western states. It was so important, in fact, that Kansas paid a bounty of two cents a pound to refiners for producing the sugar. But, despite the subsidy, the life of the industry was destined to be short.

The sorghum taste of the Kansas product was largely responsible for its failure to become a standard household product. Sugar refiners found that making white sugar out of dark brown molasses presented little difficulty but that removing the sorghum taste was almost impossible. The same drawback was found in making the brown sugars.

It was also discovered that the sweet sorghums are not as prolific as the many varieties of fodder and grain sorghum and do not withstand dry weather and insect pests as well. Nevertheless, the sweet sorghums have played an important part in

Kansas agriculture, just as the grain and forage sorghums are important crops in Kansas today. In 1882 the state produced 6,181,020 gallons of molasses. In many homes of that day sorghum molasses was the only available spread for bread, biscuits, or pancakes, so Kansas had a considerable market for the product. Molasses soon became so plentiful that commercial producers were fearful of glutting the market and forcing down the price.

Sorghum molasses was generally kept in a barrel or a keg. Someone observed that a good deal of the molasses crystallized in the bottom and along the sides of the container and concluded that it could be boiled down in the same manner as cane syrup and made into sugar. The first experiments showed that the process was easy and fairly inexpensive. The result was a boom in sugar production in Kansas.

The first record of sorghum sugar production in the state is found in the report of the Kansas Board of Agriculture for December, 1883, in which the results of operations at several points are given. Hutchinson, Kansas, reported an investment of $125,000 in its factory, the employment of 160 laborers, the growing and processing of 1,500 acres of sorghum "cane," and a centrifugal capacity of 3,200 pounds of sugar per hour with 320 gallons of syrup. Farmers were paid $1.75 a ton for delivered cane. The total amount of raw sugar produced is not stated.

At Sterling a central factory, consisting of a stone building and equipment costing $100,000, had been built by a company organized at Champaign, Illinois, as a result of experiments made by the University of Illinois. During the season covered by the report, the company processed about 14,000 tons of cane, for which they paid farmers $2.00 a ton on delivery. Here, too, only raw sugar was made, although the factory was equipped for refining.

A company at Ottawa, Kansas, produced 8,000 pounds of raw sugar and 30,000 gallons of syrup from 350 acres of cane.

The sugar was sold at eight cents a pound, but the syrup was still unsold at the time the report was made. This sugar was refined for the newly organized Lawrence Sugar Company.

The factory at Kinsley had recently been moved from Larned, and because of the recent move and a shortage of fuel, the company produced only syrup, making an average of 18 gallons from each acre of cane. The factory at Bavaria, in Saline County, had a productive capacity of 800 gallons of syrup in ten hours, cultivated 500 acres in 15 varieties of sorghum, and paid farmers $1.50 a ton for cane. Its sugar-making equipment had not been installed at the time of the report.

The factory in Liberty, Barber County, had processed 3,-500 tons of cane when production was halted by equipment failure. The price the company received for sugar was given at eight cents a pound and for syrup, 38 cents a gallon.

The report was enthusiastic about the new sugar industry and made the initial suggestion for a state bounty to foster it, quoting as precedent the bounties given in France and Germany to foster the sugar-beet industry. The report also suggested that auxiliary mills be set up to make semi-syrup for the refineries.

In 1884 the Kansas Board of Agriculture published a special report in four languages—English, German, Swedish and Danish—in compliance with an act of the state legislature for disseminating information about Kansas agriculture, horticulture, and livestock. The report included a picture of the stone sugar factory at Sterling, together with the following statement about sorghum operations in the state for the year 1883:

Acres planted in sorghum	107,042
Acres made in syrup	48,271
Acres planted for forage	53,771
Pounds of sugar made	400,000
Tons of cane manufactured	417,859
Gallons of syrup manufactured	4,684,623
Value of syrup made	$2,058,127

In the report of the board for December, 1885, it is stated that the number of sorghum sugar factories in Kansas in active operation had been reduced from five to three, and in the year of 1885 only one remained active. To explain this decrease the report stated that the cane grew just as well as formerly, and the processes had not failed, but an unprecedented and therefore impossible fall in prices of both sugar and syrup had sent the market value below the cost of production. The single factory in operation was the one at Ottawa.

Apparently a crisis had been reached in the sorghum sugar industry. On March 5, 1887, the legislature responded by providing a state bounty of two cents a pound on all sugar made in Kansas from sorghum, sugar beets, or other sugar-producing plants grown in the state. Secretary Martin Mohler of the Board of Agriculture appointed newspaper editor E. B. Cowgill as inspector to determine the amount of bounty to be paid. Under the law the inspector was not permitted to inspect manufacturing processes but was to determine the amount and sugar percentage of the product.

The inspector reported that out of a total appropriation of $15,000 in the year 1887 the following amounts were due and payable:

Parkinson Sugar Company (Fort Scott)	$7,139.44
Topeka Sugar Company	4,144.58
Conway Springs Sugar Company	1,910.58
Douglass Sugar Company	770.96
	$13,965.56

The year 1889 shows a turning point in the history of sorghum sugar production in Kansas. In the report of the board for January, 1890, records of sugar production are shown as follows:

Fort Scott	358,490 pounds
Conway Springs	267,076
Attica	267,480
Medicine Lodge	400,238
	1,293,284

Medicine Lodge is credited with being the first new company with sufficient production to pay its operating expenses.

In this report appears the first mention of sugar beets as a possible factor in the Kansas sugar industry, and the Medicine Lodge company is credited with having raised 4.7 acres of sugar beets, from which were manufactured 7,358 pounds of "firsts" and 2,800 pounds of "seconds," or a total of 10,158 pounds of sugar.

In the report of the twentieth annual meeting of the board, published in March, 1891, it is stated, "Heretofore there has been much trouble experienced by all of the companies in finding a suitable market for their product. . . . The great difficulty with sorghum is the small yield of sugar obtained." Apparently this yield averaged approximately 20 pounds of sugar to one ton of cane, though one company reported a yield of 35 pounds. However, a new method developed by the United States Department of Agriculture and experimentally applied at Fort Scott, resulted in an increased yield up to 50 pounds of sugar to one ton of cane.

H. W. Wiley, chemist for the United States Department of Agriculture, commented in the report of the board for June, 1894, on sorghum sugar production carried out under his direction at Medicine Lodge in 1893: "The investment of money during the last 15 years in sorghum sugar factories has proved almost uniformly disastrous." Medicine Lodge and Fort Scott were the only factories in operation that year.

Dr. Wiley then named the conditions under which success in sorghum sugar manufacture in Kansas might be attained:

(1) sorghum must be planted as far south as possible, (2) the seed must be carefully selected, (3) factories must be up-to-date and efficiently managed, and (4) the fiscal attitude of the government must be favorable, i.e., there must be a government subsidy.

In those far-off days, when the farmer still gathered buffalo bones and horns to sell to eke out a subsistence during the winter months, he had turned to his surest growing crop, the sweet sorghums, as a possible source of cash in sugar production. Under the influence of the promoters, he invested his meager savings in the sorghum sugar companies, voted bonds to build factories, and planted more sorghum as raw material. What the farmer did not realize was the very low percentage of sugar that could be extracted from the stalk, the imperfect methods of manufacture existing at the time, the costliness of the process, and the absence of a sure and stable market. When the state bounty was reduced in 1891 from two cents a pound to three-fourths of one cent a pound, the factories closed down and the farmer's golden dream of great wealth from his sorghum fields turned to a nightmare of disillusion.

But hope sprang forth. The sugar beet appeared, promising more sugar and cheaper processing. Through the promotion of the Board of Agriculture, alfalfa was rapidly spreading over the state. Hard winter wheat was replacing inferior varieties, the newly introduced grain sorghums were supplementing corn for the livestock industry, and the farmer was beginning to realize the value of sweet sorghum as a fodder. A dairy industry was born that was destined to become a major business.

Thus it was that a costly experiment was succeeded by agricultural prosperity based on a successful balance between farming and livestock, without which there can be no permanent system of profitable agriculture.

26: *Politics—They Played 'em Rough*

THE COURSE of Kansas politics has been marked by violent disagreements and tempestuous campaigns that rival the county-seat wars and slavery disputes of the formative years. Undoubtedly the most dangerous period in the state's history was brought about by the Populist movement of the not-so-gay nineties. The allegation that weapons were carried by members of opposing factions during this era has been denied by participants, but the fact remains that the militia was called out by the governor and deputy sheriffs stood guard about the state capitol.

The Populist movement was conceived as an organization seeking to improve the plight of the farmers, who allegedly were being victimized by money-changers, railroad magnates, and farm equipment manufacturers. It stemmed from the Farmers' Alliance, organized in Kansas in 1887, and began to take on political significance in 1890, rapidly congealing into a third-party movement that was known first as the People's party and later as the Populist party.

Most of the projects sponsored by the Populists have since become a part of the law of the land. The primary law, woman suffrage, the regulation of railroads, the supervision of stock and bond transactions, the direct election of United States senators, postal savings, the recall of public officials—all these movements were fundamental planks of the Populist party.

In 1892 the Kansas Populists waged their most bitter campaign for power, although some say the 1896 campaign was more violent. The banner was carried by L. D. Lewelling, who was elected governor; Frank Doster, who was elected to the state supreme court and was the propounder of the doctrine that "the rights of the user are paramount to the rights of the

Colonel J. W. F. Hughes
Adjutant General of Kansas and hero of the
Legislative War of 1893

owner;" Annie Diggs; Mary Elizabeth Lease (better known as Mary Ellen Lease); "Sockless" Jerry Simpson; W. F. Rightmire; and many others, most of whom were homespun orators who could make the welkin ring as it had never rung before. Theirs was a type of oratorical delivery that caused the listeners to wax furious at real and imaginary wrongs and resolve to do something about them.

The result of the 1892 campaign was Populist control of the executive branch of the state government, as well as of one important judicial position and the state senate. But it was important that they control the lower house, too. As the first count showed, sixty-five Republicans, fifty-one Populists, and one Independent were elected to the house. There remained eighteen seats which the Populists contested on the basis of fraud, illegal voting, or improper counting. By securing these seats, the Populists sought to make their control complete.

After the inauguration of Governor Lewelling and the other state officers, the legislature of 1893 proceeded to organize in a most unusual manner. The Republicans organized with George L. Douglass as speaker of the house, while the Populists organized that body with J. M. Dunsmore as speaker. The situation soon reached an impasse. The two speakers shared the dais and during part of the time slept together on the floor behind the speaker's rostrum; for in typical early-day Kansas fashion neither side would give in.

Governor Lewelling attempted to settle the matter by recognizing only the Populist house in his message to the legislature. With this official sanction, the Populists hastened to the house chambers and barred the doors to the Republicans. Then the Republicans, led by E. W. Hoch of Marion, later governor of the state, marched to the hall and broke down the doors. Today those shattered doors may be seen in the museum of the Kansas State Historical Society.

At this point the Governor called out the militia, claiming that "rioting and civil commotion were rampant about the seat of the government," although the sheriff of Shawnee County had said that he could control the situation. The fact that the sheriff had sworn in some five hundred loyal Republicans as deputies may have had something to do with the Governor's action.

Colonel J. W. F. Hughes, commander of the Third Regiment, was in St. Louis when the call came. That he was a Republican made no difference to the Governor, who gave Hughes written orders to take command of the militia and clear the hall of all except Populist members and employees. There is little doubt that Colonel Hughes prevented bloodshed by his action, in one of the most dramatic moments in the state's history. He simply put the orders in his pocket.

"Why do you not obey my orders instantly?" Governor Lewelling demanded. "Governor, the orders are illegal," replied Hughes and reinforced his assertion by contending that since the three co-ordinate branches of the government were functioning there was no authority for the militia to interfere or to dictate who were the members of the legislature. Then Colonel Hughes ordered his men to return home.

Governor Lewelling dismissed Colonel Hughes, who was later court-martialed and found guilty. Yet his actions prevented a terrible blot on the state's record. Brawls and fist fights involving hotheaded partisans who were unwilling to abide by the will of the majority had already marked the period.

Finally the question went before the state supreme court, which ruled that the Republicans and the Populists should meet separately. Thus ended the Legislative War of 1893. The Populists lost control of the executive department in the following election but returned their candidate, John W. Leedy, to the governorship in 1896 as a dying gesture. Subsequently the party ceased to play an important part in Kansas political affairs. Yet their powerful influence can still be felt in the many proposals which they introduced and which have since become active law and accepted theory.

THIS PLACE CALLED KANSAS:

IV. *Yesterday and Today*

27: *The Industrialization of Kansas*

ONE OF THE remarkable aspects of the Kansas story lies in the change in emphasis accorded agriculture and industry during the nineteen forties. For most of its life, state leaders made a studied effort to maintain Kansas as an agricultural state. Farming was looked upon as the most guileless of endeavors, and farm people were regarded as inherently chaste because of their nearness to the soil. Of course, a part of this determination also stemmed from the freight rate structure and from the belief that the population of the state was too small to support an industrial program.

As has been noted earlier, the men who wrote the Wyandotte Constitution proposed that Kansas be made a square state and that all of the plains area be given back to the Indians. The founding fathers wanted no part of the growing mining industry in the mountains or the potential livestock industry in the short-grass country. In their speeches they contended that the mining and cattle industries were incompatible with an economy based on dirt farming. There was every likelihood that a divided economy would give rise to considerable rivalry and bickering among the farmers, the cattlemen, and the miners. This was the prevalent economic theory in Kansas almost to the outbreak of World War II, a theory which precluded industrial development in Kansas for some seventy years.

It has long been known that Kansas has a large store of natural resources: lead, zinc, coal, salt, gypsum, volcanic ash, raw cement materials, natural gas, and clays and shales for brick and tile manufacturing. But, except for the flour mills, which could be found in almost every city and village in Kansas, and some salt manufacture, such industry as the state possessed was limited to the eastern one-third of the state. Milling was the only industry able to flourish under the discriminating freight rate system. Even the Kansas salt mines were unable to compete in the markets east of Chicago and St. Louis, where vast quantities of rough salt could be sold. The coal industry could move its product only two hundred miles north of the mining area, in spite of the fact that Kansas coal had exceptionally high coking qualities.

Though Kansas strongly objected to the discriminatory rates, except in the case of cement (which enjoyed a basing-point privilege) and flour (which had a milling-in-transit privilege), any Kansas manufactures were limited in market. Lead and zinc were shipped to the East only because the metals were vitally needed by eastern smelters.

One of the classic yarns about the situation concerns a large packing plant which manufactured a cleansing powder containing large quantities of volcanic ash. Since the ash was to be found in abundance in southwestern Kansas, the company proposed to build a large plant right at the source, and arrangements were made to transfer facilities and railroad tracks and to erect suitable housing for the workers. Factory plans were also completed. A traffic expert happened in on the final conference on the project. He listened for a while, then asked the group to delay further action until he could investigate the rate structure. Later he reported that if the factory were built in Kansas it would cost eleven cents per can to manufacture and transport the product to the concentrated markets east of the Mississippi River. At the time, the product was selling at ten cents per can, and the manufacturer, the jobbers, and the retailers were enjoying a substantial profit. The pumice, as raw material, could be shipped at a very low rate from the mines to the factories, but the rate for the manufactured product would be prohibitive. The factory was never built.

At one time Kansas had a large glass-manufacturing industry, but it was choked off many years ago by the same discriminatory practices mentioned above. Packing plants in Kansas City and subsidiary soap factories using the packers' wastes and fats did form the nucleus of an industry at an early stage.

Kansas became the largest milling center of the nation by reason of favorable freight rates, which were classed under a so-called milling-in-transit privilege providing that wheat grown in Kansas and started on its way to market can be stopped at any point along the natural route for processing and then delivered to the mills, where it may be further processed into flour, bran, shorts, and other products. Then it may continue in the same general direction at the original rate. Obviously, the entire Kansas milling industry might very well be destroyed if this privilege were removed.

It is to Kansas' credit that its people did something about the situation. In the Republican platform of 1938 the party insisted that Kansas seek new industries for the state and establish a commission to promote the interest of outside industry. When the Republicans won the election, they proceeded to create the Kansas Industrial Development Commission, which set about its assigned task and within ten years was able to announce that 117 new industries had begun operations in Kansas and that the aggregate expenditures for industrial contracts and plant expansion would amount to eighty million dollars during the single year 1949.

One of the first acts of the new commission was to assign five thousand dollars of its grant to a study of the freight rate problem, which seemed to be the major obstacle to industry. This study proved the contention that not only Kansas but at least seven other states in the immediate area suffered from rate discrimination. North Dakota, South Dakota, Nebraska, Kansas, Oklahoma, Arkansas, and Texas, as well as several southern states, were shipping under an unequal rate system. In classifying the articles shipped from the area, the commission discovered that freight rates varied widely within three large general territories, Official (Eastern), Southern, and Western.

After a conference held by the governors of the seven western states, steps were taken to present a solid front to the western railroads and the eastern states. The case was carried to the Interstate Commerce Commission, which directed railroads to prepare and publish a uniform classification throughout the nation. The United States Supreme Court upheld the decision of the I.C.C. The result was a rate scale lowered by about 35 per cent in the area east of the Rocky Mountains and raised by about 15 per cent in the Official Territory. Thus Kansas led again in improving a serious situation.

The subsequent industrial development in Kansas prompted the commission to seek to improve the poor tourist record of the state. Their efforts overcame the reluctance of tourists to drive across the state and also persuaded employers to send workers and their families into Kansas.

One of the main objectives of the body was to exploit and utilize the enormous mineral resources. Today, the total mineral production in Kansas, including the lead, zinc, salt, coal, rock, shale, oil, and gas production, exceeds the value of the livestock industry, the largest single source of agricultural revenue. By mid-century there was greater activity in oil exploration and production than at any other time in history, and natural-gas production had become a multimillion dollar industry.

While there was a reduction in the output of coal, lead, and zinc, the brick, cement, gypsum, tile, and stone industries showed marked increases, and many small manufacturing concerns in countless towns were flourishing in local and national markets.

With regard to labor, there is a distinct trend toward a decreased rural population and an increased urban population. Farm operations have not suffered, however, because mechanical aids have replaced the many farm hands once required to maintain a large crop production. Kansas farms are larger, incomes are greater, its towns are more prosperous—but not because of foresight on the part of its founders. Indeed, despite predictions to the contrary, Kansas has successfully balanced and amalgamated farming, mining, and cattle-raising and has, moreover, proved itself as an industrial commonwealth.

28: *The Grasshopper Scourge*

THE GRASSHOPPER and the chinch bug have been the two most destructive invaders of Kansas farm fields. The chinch bug was conquered many years ago, but the grasshopper continues to destroy growing crops in large areas of the state each year despite every scientific control known to man.

The worst infestation came in August, 1874, when practically the entire state was denuded of every blade of grass and all other vegetation. The grasshoppers invaded without warning and remained until there was nothing left to feed on. Before they departed, they deposited their eggs in Kansas soil, and in the spring of 1875 hordes of the insects hatched out. However, they moved on in time for the farmers to replant, and the terrible situation of the previous year was not repeated.

Ferdinand J. Funk came to Kansas in May, 1874, with the Mennonites from Germany. His father, believing that it was good business to buy a farm already in cultivation, bought eighty acres of wheatland in Marion County and harvested the crop. Funk, a boy of fourteen at the time, has described the afternoon of August 6, 1874:

There was not a hint of a cloud in the sky that day until along about four o'clock in the afternoon. Then the sky suddenly became hazy and speedily darkened until in a matter of a few minutes it was so dark that it not only frightened me but did something to the chickens. I can't say they were frightened. But they hastened to their roosts as fast as they could.

It hit my youthful mind as if some terrible and disastrous catastrophe was impending that could transform the brightest sort of a day into the blackness of night in a few minutes.

Then with a whizzing, whirring sound the grasshoppers came from the northwest and in unbelievable numbers. They lit on everything. I was covered from head to foot. When they hit my face or hands the impact was like missiles and at once the insects began to eat. The ground was covered, in some spots to a depth of three or four inches, and trees along the creek were so loaded with grasshoppers that large limbs were broken off. The insects fell into the creek and drowned and the dead insects were in such numbers that they formed a dam and the water turned brown and our cattle and horses would not drink it. Even fish died in the foul water.

It was only a few minutes that darkness prevailed. Then the hoppers were all out of the sky and eating. The chickens came out of the hen house and gorged themselves on hoppers and then stood around sad eyed that they could not eat more.

We had about fifteen acres of corn which older settlers said would make fifty bushels an acre. The hoppers landed about four o'clock. By dark there wasn't a stalk of that field of corn over a foot high left in the entire field. I slept in a straw stack. That night the hoppers ate my straw hat, or most of it, leaving me only a part of the brim and a part of the crown. They seemed to like sweaty things and ate around the sweatband of my hat. They gnawed the handles of pitchforks and other farm tools that had absorbed per-

166

spiration and they ate the harness on the horses or hanging in the barn. They ate every leaf off the trees and every green thing on our farm except the grass. They didn't eat much of that.[1]

There were several grasshopper invasions in Kansas prior to 1874. The *Annals of Kansas*[2] records a reference to grasshoppers "clouding" the sky above Kansas and Missouri as early as 1820. In 1854 Father John Schoenmachers of the Osage Indian Mission, near present St. Paul, Kansas, reported a grasshopper raid in which the insects "came down like a fall of snow." In the spring of 1855 a new crop of grasshoppers destroyed all the crops along the Neosho River and ate the grass in the vicinity of the mission. In 1860 the *Emporia News* reported grasshoppers "by the millions" in and around Emporia.

For many years the "hopper-dozer" was the favorite weapon against the grasshopper. This machine was mounted on wheels and was equipped with two or three boards across the bottom and a backstop made of canvas. Immediately in front of the backstop was a trough containing kerosene. The dozer was pulled by horses hitched at either end, and as the grasshoppers hit the backstop they fell into the kerosene.

Then chemists at the Kansas State Agricultural College discovered the grasshoppers' fondness for dampened bran. They mixed poisons with the bran and spread it in fields where no domestic animals were allowed to graze. This treatment was soon found to be effective.

In the Kansas Historical Society may be found letters from early-day settlers telling how the grasshoppers ate all the leaves and fruit on the peach trees and left only the peach stones and the hardier wood of the old branches. Other letters say that the grasshoppers got into the houses and ate window curtains and bedclothing. It is unfortunate that photography was in its infancy at that time. So far as the Kansas Historical Society is able

[1] Written for the author from personal notes of F. J. Funk.
[2] By Daniel W. Wilder (New ed., Topeka, T. D. Thacher, 1886).

to learn, there is not a single authentic photograph of the grasshopper invasion of 1874, and there are only a few sketches of the denuded landscape as it appeared after the insect pests had gone their way.

As soon as the extent of the damage was learned, Governor Thomas A. Osborn was importuned by members of the legislature and the Republican state convention to call the lawmakers into emergency session (incidentally, the first special session held in Kansas). Since it was too late in the year to plant new crops, the farmers and townspeople were faced with starvation, not only for their livestock but for themselves.

The legislature met on September 15, 1874. The session lasted for only a week and passed few measures except those having to do with relief bonds. One bill authorized the state to issue $73,000 in bonds for relief purposes. But it was stipulated that these bonds should be issued only to buy the state's bonds, after which the money would be issued to the stricken counties in exchange for their relief bonds. Another bill authorized each of the counties to issue relief bonds up to $5,000. Nineteen counties voted to issue bonds to take care of the needy citizens, and *The Annals of Kansas* says that bonds totaling $7,500 were issued before the state supreme court declared the laws invalid.

Thus much of the effort of the special session was wasted. The state was unable to issue the bonds, and the counties could not sell their bonds except at heavy discounts. The banks and bond brokers would not take emergency warrants except at heavy discounts. So the money available for relief was limited to the small amounts in the county poor funds.

Thousands of Kansans returned to their former homes in other states during the winter and returned the next year to plant their crops. The large number of farmers who did not have the money to leave the state were cared for by private charities.

A central relief committee, supervised by state officials, was organized and made an appeal to eastern states for aid for the farmers. An official audit of the committee's work made a year later shows that a total of 124 carloads of food and clothing and $20,713 in cash were received. The 12,160 boxes and barrels of food and clothing were valued at $110,600. In addition, the army gave 4,541 blankets, 1,834 heavy winter overcoats, 131 sack coats, 135 pairs of trousers, and 4,468 pairs of boots. Other easterners sent food and clothing to their families and friends in Kansas. It has been unofficially estimated that the total relief in the afflicted areas of Kansas amounted to about $500,000.

Beginning with the special session in 1874 members of the legislature gave consideration to various plans for preventing another devastation by the grasshoppers. In 1877 the legislature enacted the famous "Grasshopper Army" law, which was never enforced but remained in effect until the general statutes were revised in 1923.

The "Grasshopper Army" law is a classic among legal documents, and it has often been asserted that no similar law has ever been enacted in the United States. The law is quoted in part below.

SEC. 1. That the township trustees of the different townships, and the mayors of cities which are not included in any township of any county within this state, are hereby authorized, and it is made their duty, when so requested in writing by fifteen of the legal voters of the township or city, to issue orders to the road overseers of the different road districts within their respective townships or cities, to warn out all able-bodied male citizens between the ages of twelve and sixty-five years, within their respective districts, for the purpose of destroying locusts or migratory grasshoppers.

SEC. 2. It shall be the duty of road overseers, immediately after receiving said order, to proceed at once to warn out all persons liable under section 1 of this act, giving notice of the time and place of meeting, and the tools to be used, and the kind of work expected to be performed; and all work shall be done and performed under the direction of the road overseers.

Other sections authorized the entry of the grasshopper armies upon any threatened land and directed the secretary of the state board of agriculture to compile a pamphlet listing the most effective ways of fighting or controlling grasshoppers and to provide ten copies of the pamphlet to each township trustee.

Another law passed by the 1877 legislature authorized counties in the same senatorial district to hold joint campaigns to fight the insects. Senatorial districts could hold joint campaigns in the same manner. The law specifically provided that if the grasshoppers were newly hatched they could be driven from the fields into open grasslands and burned.

Some years later, when the bran mash method proved successful in ridding the fields of the insects, the legislature authorized the various counties to help provide poison for the mixture.

Of course, many tall tales were told about the great scourge. Grasshopper eggs were used on at least one occasion as a substitute for cash. As the story goes, William H. Fulcomer gathered a gallon of the insect eggs and took them to the office of James C. Humphrey, editor of the *Belleville Telescope*. Fulcomer was in arrears on his newspaper subscription and offered the eggs as payment. Humphrey accepted them as full credit.

Frank Carpenter, a farmer at Copeland, had believed that the grasshoppers lived on green salads, since they seemed to concentrate on leaves and stalks. While working in his field one day he lost his wallet, and when it was found he discovered that grasshoppers had eaten a hole through the leather and consumed a considerable portion of two ten-dollar bills and one one-dollar bill.

On one occasion a group of farmers bought turkeys and took them to their grasshopper-infested alfalfa fields. They had to give up the project, however, because the turkeys came squawking back to the farmhouses begging for protection. The grasshoppers had stripped them clean of feathers and picked holes through the skin. Scientists have since declared this story to be preposterous, but there can be no doubt about the truth of the other tales.

29: *From Saloons to Bootleggers to Bottle Stores*

FOR SIXTY-NINE years (1880–1949) the Kansas constitution prohibited the manufacture, sale, or gift of all forms of intoxicating liquor. Furthermore, for the last thirty years of that period the state went a step farther and maintained statutory prohibition against even the possession of liquor, and the contests to keep or repeal the laws and constitutional provisions have been almost perennial.

Most certainly, such a stringent clamp on the thirsts and habits of generations of citizens might be expected to occasion the spilling of a little blood—and considerable liquor. It was not expected, however, that a "Bone Dry" law, such as was enacted by the legislature of 1915, would have the effect of making criminals of a large segment of the population. This was not the intent of the sponsors of the law, who stated their aim as solely to punish bootleggers.

Thus the "Bone Dry" law was the actual target of the repeal campaign of 1948, when the legislature voted to resubmit the prohibition question to the voters. Several members of the legislature asserted that the repeal of this one law would have satisfied the wets. However, observers say that the very pressure which had been used so successfully by the drys for sixty-nine years caused the wholesale repeal of prohibition, both statutory and constitutional.

The adoption of the constitutional amendment in 1880 was not a sudden whim. Action came suddenly in the legislature of 1879 only because some attempted political chicanery backfired. The agitation for prohibition had begun long before Kansas became a state. The Independent Order of Good Templars, a temperance organization, had been working toward this objective since early territorial days and continued its agitation until constitutional prohibition was an accomplished fact.

At each of the four constitutional conventions the proposal was made that prohibition be included in the constitution. Three of the conventions flatly rejected the proposal. The Wyandotte Convention neither rejected nor adopted the proposal, although two efforts were made to table the section, action which would have been tantamount to rejection. Both efforts failed. When the matter came before the group a third time, Solon O. Thacher, member from Lawrence, made a short speech which resulted in a no-action decision on the part of the convention. He pointed out that prohibiting the liquor traffic might become as explosive a problem as prohibiting slavery had been and that including two such touchy subjects in the constitution could easily result in the rejection of the document by Congress. He added that settlers in the territory might also reject the constitution and force another convention. These sound arguments led the members to let the matter rest.

The temperance agitators renewed their campaign with greater vigor after Kansas was admitted to the Union in 1861. The resolution was submitted to both houses at every legislative session from 1861 until 1879, when the necessary votes were finally obtained.

It may be noted here that during the year 1879 Governor John P. St. John, the prohibition governor and one of the leaders of the temperance movement, had urged the legislature to submit the amendment to the people. He told the body that

(above) Carry Nation (at right) in action in Enterprise, Kansas
(below) Carry Nation escorted by the sheriff of Enterprise

he would always favor prohibition but that he did not desire the passage of a law which would not be enforced. The Governor then specifically suggested that the "dram-shop law" of 1868, which provided for regulation and licensing of saloons and other dispensaries, be amended to permit greater control.

The resolution on the constitutional amendment was offered in the senate and remained with the committee on temperance until very late in the session. In the meantime, the house of representatives had passed the stringent dram-shop law as proposed by the governor and sent it to the senate, where it joined the prohibition resolution in the committee on temperance.

It was here that the liquor lobby saw a chance to kill both projects in the 1879 session. First, it persuaded the senate committee to bring out both projects and move that the amendment be considered first. The lobbyists had been told that the house certainly would not adopt such a resolution, so they hurried it through the senate in order to tangle the two measures in the last-minute jam in the house. The senate unanimously adopted the resolution. The shock came a few days later when the resolution was brought up in the house. The temperance group, led by J. R. Detwiler of the Osage mission, had been circulating petitions and applying pressure with organized zeal. The struggle between the two factions was extremely close and bitter. When the roll call was ordered the count showed that the resolution lacked only one vote of the necessary two-thirds majority. Mrs. G. W. Greevey, wife of a member from Wyandotte County, a former schoolteacher, and an active temperance worker, listened to the debate and watched her husband vote against submission of the amendment. She then left the gallery and went down on the house floor to her husband's desk, argued briefly, and told him that "this is a moral question on which the people should be allowed to express their views." Representative Greevey changed his vote, much to the consternation of the liquor interests, the resolution was adopted, and thus constitutional prohibition was submitted to the people.

The next day Governor St. John invited Mrs. Greevey to come to his office, where in the presence of a considerable number of active prohibitionists he presented her with a scroll declaring her to be "The Mother of Prohibition in Kansas."

The campaign for adoption of the amendment by the people, one of the most colorful campaigns in the annals of Kansas, really began in February, 1880, when Mrs. Drusilla Wilson and her husband started out from Lawrence in their surrey. They visited almost every county in the state, and Mrs. Wilson made from two to twenty speeches in each county. Wherever she found a group of women, especially girls, gathered together she talked about the evils of strong drink and organized clubs to promote the temperance cause. She did not cease to campaign until election day.

A great prohibition rally was held at Bismarck Grove, near Lawrence, in August. It was reported that 25,000 people attended. Governor St. John and a dozen or more of the best-known temperance speakers from all parts of the country came to the rally and helped arouse the citizenry to the need for curbing the evils of strong drink. Meetings were held in churches and schoolhouses, and the campaign increased in intensity throughout September and October. In this campaign Solon Thacher actively supported prohibition.

The amendment was adopted by a vote 92,302 to 84,304. (Women did not yet have the right to vote.) The legislature of 1881 passed the enabling laws, and a parade was held in Topeka on May 1 by the saloon keepers and their friends, who gathered up what liquor remained, paraded to the statehouse, and set out a "prohibition tree" on the grounds. Everybody poured liquor into the hole to water the tree. No one seems to remember now which tree the prohibition tree happens to be.

The Republican party was always the staunch supporter of prohibition. While it seldom declared against resubmission of the amendment to the people, it consistently reaffirmed its support of strict enforcement of the law. The Democrats elected Governor G. W. Glick in 1882 on a resubmission platform and were aided by the fact that Governor St. John was the Republican nominee for a third term as governor. From 1882 until 1906 the Democratic party regularly declared for the resubmission of the prohibitory amendment. When Colonel W. A. Harris agreed to become the Democratic candidate for governor in 1906, he demanded that the resubmission plank be taken out of the platform, and it was not restored until 1946.

The amendment was resubmitted by a Republican legislature in 1933 and voted on in 1934. In that year the people defeated repeal by a vote of 436,688 to 347,644. In 1946 both parties agreed that the people should vote again on the proposition, and the Republican legislature of 1947 adopted a resolution to submit to the people an amendment barring saloons but permitting the sale of bottled liquor. The vote was 422,294 for the new amendment to 358,310 for constitutional prohibition. Only 45 of the 105 counties of the state voted wet. The 1949 legislature then enacted laws to regulate and control bottle stores.

The exploits of Mrs. Carry Nation, Mrs. Myra McHenry, and other women who took it upon themselves to enforce the constitution by personally wrecking saloons and emptying liquor barrels, played a prominent part in the background. Their raids had the effect of crystallizing determination to enforce the laws and close liquor establishments. A number of city officials were ousted from office because of their failure to enforce the law.

Mrs. Nation's raids were not the first in Kansas. The precedent for her raids had been established nearly fifty years before. Although neglected by history, a raid was staged by a group of Topekans July 4, 1855, when the city was only six months old. The town association had adopted a rule that none of the original town lots could be used as the site for a liquor establishment. Lawrence, Baldwin, and nearly every other city organized in Kansas in the early days had adopted similar prohibitions.

But Topeka, unincorporated as yet and lacking a city government, had no way of enforcing the prohibition. So when a group of the founders discovered that a saloon had been opened on one of the original lots of the town, they gathered up axes and sledge hammers, went to the building, and smashed everything in the place, simultaneously serving a warning on the owner that the process would be repeated if he opened again.

A short time later a druggist at Big Springs brought to his store a keg of whisky, which he proposed to give away, a cup at a time, on Saturday night. The crowd had gathered and was smacking its collective lips in anticipation, when a group of men walked in, rolled the keg into the road, knocked in the head, and let the liquor flow into a pile of shavings and sawdust which had been brought to the scene in the aprons of their womenfolk. Then the pile was set afire.

Of course, the saloons were operating because many citizens in the more populous communities were not in sympathy with the law. In some towns saloons were allowed to operate openly and were simply fined every month. In 1905, twenty-four years after the state became dry, 250 saloons were counted in Kansas City alone, and until 1908 druggists needed no more than the testimony of the "patient" to sell a medicinal dosage. In that year the law was stiffened, and in 1909 the legislature removed the provision which permitted sales for medicinal purposes.

But despite these illuminating sidelights, the vital issue throughout the years of Kansas prohibition seems to have been whether the measures of restraint, and finally total obliteration, were helping to create a temperate people. For as the restrictions on liquor traffic became more stringent, efforts to obtain and deliver the product became more concerted. Indeed, it is a significant feature of Kansas history that on this question the minority refused to be ruled by the will of the majority. A difference of only 5 per cent of the votes in 1880 could have changed the entire course of prohibition history. And Kansas became wet again when only 8 per cent of the votes of 1948 spelled the margin.

Thus have Kansans treated the prohibition question, drinking quietly or openly as the current law dictated, spiking non-alcoholic beer with alcohol when the cost of bootleg whisky was too high, manufacturing "deep shaft" and home-brew in mine shafts and basements, and at the same time witnessing fervent dry campaigns of spectacular proportions.

What the future holds can not be forecast. The past, from saloons to bootleggers to bottle stores, has been stimulating.

30: *Gold in the Hills*

O N TWO occasions shouts of joy at the discovery of gold have resounded across the bluffs, hilltops, and valleys of Kansas. The first discovery was made in 1858 in present Colorado when the Territory of Kansas extended westward to the Continental Divide. The second discovery was made well within the present confines of the state. This event occurred just before the turn of the century, and for a period of seven or eight years thereafter countless tons of shale were mined and millions of dollars were spent on mills, equipment, and labor.

Much of the exploited area has since been covered by water from the Cedar Bluff dam, but there are ample records of the prospecting that took place along the Smoky Hill River in Ellis and Trego counties.

The headquarters of the gold prospectors was Chetolah, southwest of Hays in Ellis County. During the heyday of the rush Chetolah sported a large hotel, several business buildings, and a creditable residential section. The town collapsed when the mining companies departed, revived for about a year during the oil boom, and then faded from the map.

The theory that precious metals could be obtained from the shale in western Kansas was originated by Cyrus K. Holliday in 1895. Mr. Holliday knew that in 1848 a government expedition had explored western Kansas and had reported the presence of minerals of some kind in the valley of the Smoky River in present Ellis County. There are many references to gold-hunting in the mountains of Kansas during the early days. A resident of Monroe County, Wisconsin, had written on December 29, 1858, to his relatives in New England:

If any of the folks want to come west it will be a good time this spring for there will be a great rush for the Kansas gold mines where they think they can pick up gold in abundance. But many of them, I think, will be glad before one year rolls around to sell their gold to get back, but will not find a purchaser.

Many "processes" for proving gold were invented. The metallurgical charlatan was always on hand, with a parasitic process which extracted gold only from his employers. The expert ore "salter" was at work. Frauds and swindlers attracted by the growing excitement soon gave the area such a bad name that men owning shale land were ashamed to admit it. Newspapers sarcastically dubbed the shale owners "shale-ionaires." Fraudulent companies issued attractive advertising matter and attempted to sell worthless stock to credulous investors.

But there was an element of truth in all this welter of misrepresentation and chicanery, and under Holliday's leadership twenty-six wealthy and thoroughly responsible Topeka businessmen set about proving the existence of gold.

A report of the Kansas Academy of Science states:

The late Cyrus K. Holliday, led by reports and traditions, joined with a Mr. Stotz in outfitting a prospector named Ephriam Baker, who explored the region (along the Smoky Hill west of Fort Hays) and obtained samples which were sent to Chicago and Denver for Assay. One of the certificates reports a value of gold of $32 and silver 25 cents per ton.

Soon after Holliday's venture Ernest Fahrig of Philadelphia developed his electrolytic process for extracting gold. Professor Fahrig, head of the laboratories of the Philadelphia museum, resigned his position in 1899 to come to Kansas to demonstrate his new process along the Smoky Hill River. He built a mill in Topeka, which produced some gold and remained in operation for two years. The process proved successful and is now generally used in extracting gold and other metals from shales and sea water.

However, the chief disadvantage in the Kansas gold fields was that, while small pockets of the precious metal were found and once in a while a ton of the shales would bring forth from fifteen to twenty dollars in real gold, the next two thousand tons of shale from the same pit might produce nothing.

J. T. Lovewell of Washburn College made a number of assays of the Kansas shales, while other chemists and metallurgists made every test known to the gold industry. Most of them found traces of gold and silver, but the widely varying reports made by these experts finally resulted in the failure of the gold mining ventures in Kansas.

In a report to the Kansas Academy of Science, Professor Lovewell wrote:

Without undertaking to determine how the gold got into the shale, whether by precipitation from the sea water or by alluvial deposits, it is certainly in a very fine state of division. When the shale is pulverized to 100-mesh and carefully washed with water a residue is found, which under the microscope shows grains of silica and pyrite and some grains of gold. Some residue yields a quantity of gold on assay, which shows that plain washing with water will produce considerable concentration of values. In the washing process it is likely that we lose some of the very finely divided gold.

In my investigation of this shale many modes of assays have been tried. The ore has been roasted with various kinds of fluxes before assay and in a good many cases this preliminary treatment has been useful. In the spring of 1899, co-operating with Doctor Franklin, [a chemist at the University of Kansas] at Lawrence we made over 100 assays of shale, which had been obtained from a number of different places. Many of our results were blanks, but a few showed small values of gold. In the following summer I took shale from many places up and down the river for several miles.

I brought my specimens to Topeka and worked on them for a month, making over 100 assays. This gave small values, the last twenty averaging about one dollar to the ton. In these two series of assays the number of blanks were greater than the number which showed values, but the shales were taken from all parts of the formations, and many of them doubtless contained no gold. Since then I have made many hundreds of assays and I suppose the average values obtained were two to three dollars a ton. One series of 66 assays gave an average of $2.58 per ton. In my laboratory, recently, by concentration methods, 144 assays gave an average of $13.52 per ton.

In the same report Professor Lovewell said:

The most puzzling part of the investigation is that from the same pulp, mixed as carefully as we know how to do it, very discordant values will appear. They have varied as much as fifty dollars per ton.

It would appear, therefore, that the gold is not uniformly distributed and unwittingly, in taking our assay, we get a rich portion one time and a lean portion at another time. Also, owing to the unknown and peculiar conditions of the ore, very likely to its fine divisions, the values in one case are led away by heavy vapors, while in another instance the values are in some way retained.

F. H. Blake, a New York mining engineer, collected twenty-five samples of the shale at different points along the Smoky Hill River and had the assays made in Denver. Six samples contained no trace of gold, ten showed small traces, and nine ranged in value from twenty cents to sixteen dollars a ton.

S. B. Edwards, a Colorado mining expert, made nineteen assays, which showed an average value of $2.08 a ton. The individual assays varied from $0.42 to $18.78 a ton.

One of the largest of the gold-mining companies was the Kansas Pioneer Gold Shale Company, formed in Topeka and incorporated in South Dakota. The company had a capital of two and one-half million dollars, and shares of stock, "fully paid and nonassessable," sold at ten cents a share. Promoted by capitalists in Kansas and Texas, the company owned about two thousand acres of land along the Smoky Hill River, some fifteen miles southwest of Hays. A mill had been installed at Chetolah by Dr. Charles H. Gage, a mining chemist from Denver, who told the promoters that even if the gold averaged only one dollar to the ton the great volume of shale going through the mill would insure a profit.

A glance at the list of officers and directors of the Kansas Pioneer Gold Shale Company reveals the names of several prominent Kansas citizens:

OFFICERS

President	D. R. Beatty, Beaumont, Texas
Vice-president	C. E. Foote, Topeka, Kansas
Secretary	M. S. Waller, Denver, Colorado
General attorney	Colonel J. H. Richards, Fort Scott, Kansas
General manager	Carl Moller, St. Louis, Missouri
General auditor	W. B. Sharp, Dallas, Texas

BOARD OF DIRECTORS

H. J. Penney, Hays, Kansas
George M. Noble, Topeka, Kansas
G. E. Ross-Lewin, Denver, Colorado
D. R. Beatty, Beaumont, Texas
C. E. Foote, Topeka, Kansas
M. S. Waller, Denver, Colorado
Carl Moller, St. Louis, Missouri

ADVISORY BOARD

The Honorable Frank Doster, Marion, Kansas
J. R. Mulvane, Topeka, Kansas
Colonel J. H. Richards, Fort Scott, Kansas

C. E. Foote was president of the largest municipal bond house in Kansas at the time. Colonel Richards was the legal representative for the Missouri Pacific Railroad in Kansas and was prominent in Republican political affairs in the state. H. J. Penney was vice-president of the Citizens State Bank and the mayor of Hays. George M. Noble was president of the largest real estate and insurance firm in Topeka. Frank Doster was chief justice of the Kansas supreme court. J. R. Mulvane was a founder and the president of the Bank of Topeka (now the National Bank of Topeka).

C. J. Lantry and a group of friends also built a mill, which was operated by Professor Fahrig. At that time the Lantry brothers were the most prominent construction contractors in Kansas. They owned and operated stone quarries around Strong City and built large sections of the Santa Fé Railway in Kansas and other states.

These and other companies proved that the stories of gold were not merely prospectors' or promoters' yarns. But the gold occurred in such small quantities and the expense of milling was so great that no profit could ever be hoped for. Gradually the companies disbanded, and only a few empty buildings remained as monuments to the high hopes of the prospectors.

A few years ago the last of the gold mills on the Smoky Hill River burned, and Chetolah, once bustling and active, is now a ghost town.

3 1 : *Mineral Springs, but No Spas*

EXPLOITATION of the mineral springs in Kansas was almost as extensive as the promotion of paper towns by the boomers. It may be that the mineral-springs business in Kansas was even better (and certainly it was more tangible) than selling corner lots in nonexisting towns that *hoped* to get a railroad and *promised* to become county seats.

Kansas does have a large number of mineral springs, some of which have considerable therapeutic value. At one time there were many flourishing health resorts and luxurious hotels devoted to the exploitation of the sickly elite who came to take the baths and drink the waters. Some of the structures are still standing, faded and weather-beaten reminders of a day when people still believed in miracles.

The promoters of the mineral springs circulated elaborate lithographs showing the development work which had been undertaken to accommodate those seeking health-giving waters. The promoters, most of them medical quacks of the first order, published fairly accurate chemical analyses of the water but failed to add that the curative minerals were offset by purgative minerals too powerful for the human body to stand. In time this factor was bound to spell doom for the health resorts.

Kansas newspapers published fifty to seventy years ago show countless advertisements urging those afflicted with any of a number of diseases to come to the springs, live in the hotel (elaborately illustrated), and bathe in the springs or drink the

waters as prescribed by the "doctor" in residence. The operators also offered to ship bottles of the water to those who would
pay the price.

These advertisements were only slightly less flamboyant
than the claims the medicine men made for the vile liquids they
sold at one dollar a bottle, or six bottles for five dollars. While
the mineral-springs promoters did not guarantee that the waters
would grow hair and stop men from chewing tobacco, they
did make claims that were extravagant, to say the least. One
"doctor," who owned a large hotel and operated a system of
springs, claimed that the mineral waters had "never failed to
to cure after doctors had failed" and stated that the water
would cure dyspepsia, insomnia, rheumatism, kidney ailments,
dropsy, heart throbbings, "that tired feeling," and other real
or fancied ailments. In truth, some of the waters were so evil-
smelling that they would seem capable of curing a broken leg
simply by proximity. Yet patients would hold their noses, take
a few swallows, sputter, choke, and a few days later compose
ringing letters extolling the wonderful restorative powers of
the treatment.

By the turn of the century Kansas was dotted with health
resorts. If one could believe the advertising, those afflicted with
flat feet, bunions, indigestion, sciatica, lumbago, headaches,
liver spots, or aching muscles had only to "take the treatment"
to be cured. Even as late as 1912 state officials were succumb-
ing to the various testimonials, and the state paid out a good
deal of money for bottles of water installed in the offices.

Many of the boomers believed that because of the wide
variety of minerals in the various springs Kansas was destined
to become the great American health resort. The state legislature, aroused at length by the barrage of advertising and pro-
motional material, directed the state geological survey to make
a complete investigation of all mineral-springs resorts in the
state. In 1903 a special appropriation was made for the survey,
and additional state funds were allocated to promote those

springs which were found to have genuine therapeutic value.

E. H. S. Bailey, chairman of the chemistry department of the University of Kansas, was to make the chemical analyses, and Erasmus Haworth, head of the geological survey, a conscientious and careful workman, saw to it that each spring was carefully inspected and that the samples of water were not subject to contamination.

Eight types of springs were found to be in operation in the state. The following list shows the chemical classification of the springs and the number of springs in each group:

Chloride group	17 *springs*
Sulfate	23
Chlor-sulfate	9
Carbonate	14
Chlor-carbonate	7
Sulfid	9
Chalybeate	12
Special (miscellaneous)	6

Eleven springs which contained no measurable quantities of minerals were classed as soft-water springs.

More springs were exploited than were listed in the different groups. At some points as many as a half-dozen springs containing varying quantities of minerals were operated as one system.

Several doctors assisted in the survey, among them a large number whose patients had deserted them for the promises of the various health resorts, only to return in worse condition, both physically and financially.

The survey published a detailed report, which resulted in a sudden exodus from the state of large numbers of promoters, who moved on to greener pastures.

The best known mineral springs in the state were the Waconda Springs in Mitchell County, commonly called the Great Spirit Springs. Of this group the report said:

Contrary to local belief the Waconda Springs are in no way volcanic and neither do they have any connection with the ocean. They are merely artesian springs and the water is mineralized because it comes from the saliferous shale lying at the top of the Dakota. Drilled wells penetrating this formation produce water of the same type.

By precipitation of the less soluble compounds which the waters carry in solution has built up a mound 42 feet high with a diameter at the base of 300 feet and at the top 150 feet. The top is nearly flat, with a craterlike depression in the center 35 feet deep and about 54 feet across. This depression is filled with water but overflow is rare, due to escape of the water through openings in the flanks of the mound.

A well-known Indian legend about the Waconda Springs lent color and romance to the spot and was at least partly responsible for the success of the resort. As the legend goes, the young son of a chief fell in love with a beautiful maiden of a hostile tribe. The warriors of the hostile tribe found the lovers at the springs and killed the boy in the presence of the maiden, who thereupon threw herself into the water and drowned.

Merrill Springs was one of the first health resorts. The large hotel has long been a landmark on U. S. Highway 75, about fifteen miles south of Topeka and three miles north of Carbondale. The resort was a favorite week-end gathering place for legislators, politicians, and lobbyists, who took the train to Carbondale and were picked up there by a large omnibus drawn by four horses and taken to the springs. The hotel was built by M. D. Merrill and was managed by Dr. H. H. Swallow until the nineteen twenties. Since that time the hotel stood vacant and was torn down at mid-century.

Several efforts have been made in recent years to revive the popularity of some of the better mineral springs in the state. But it appears that the people of Kansas are too healthy to require the revitalizing benefits of mineral-spring water, and most of these efforts have proved unsuccessful.

3 2: *Sentiment and Tradition*

ONLY RARELY do sentiment and tradition win a bout with hardheaded government officials. But it has happened in Kansas on at least one occasion, when the federal committee on geographic names officially decreed that the Osage River would henceforth be called the Marais des Cygnes. It wasn't just a whim that prompted a few Kansans to make the long campaign to restore the original name of the river. According to history and tradition, Indians and traders had called it by the French name long before it became known as the Osage River.

The river rises in southeastern Wabaunsee and northern Lyon counties and is formed by the junction of 142-Mile Creek[1] and Elm Creek, northeast of Emporia. A number of theories about the origin of the name have been advanced. According to the French traders who moved into Kansas, the river was known to the Indians as the "Marsh of the Swans" because great numbers of the birds could be found in the region each spring and fall. According to A. E. Shirling,

Marais des Cygnes was the name given by the Indians to a tribal gathering place where the Little Osage joins the Marais des Cygnes. The Indian name mi-xa-cka-u-tsi means the spot abounding in wild swans. So, the French called it Marais des Cygnes, the marsh of the swans and applied the name to the entire river. In earlier days when trumpeter swans flew across country in long, waving lines, the sluggish Marais des Cygnes probably was a favorite place for swans as well as Indians, and the name Marsh of the Swans was appropriate. But it has been many a year since that river reflected the graceful, curving neck of a swan.

[1] It was a common practice among explorers, traders, and army detachments to assign numbers rather than names to the creeks and small streams they encountered.

In his *History of the State of Kansas*, published in 1883, T. A. Andreas noted that the "northern fork of the Osage was called the Marais des Cygnes until its junction with the Little Osage, the two forks uniting to form the Osage." Andreas continued:

> In the fall of 1820, two Presbyterian Missions were established among the Osages by the United Foreign Missionary Society, Union Station on the Neosho, and Harmony Station. . . . Harmony Station was situated on the Marais des Cygnes River, six miles above its junction with the Osage, about fifteen miles east from the western line of the state of Missouri and the same distance from the village of the Great Osages on the Osage River. The buildings of the establishment were erected on the margin of the Marais des Cygnes, "a specious and handsome green in front, and in the rear a vast prairie covered with grass." The mill site belonging to the mission, and the United States trading house, were a mile below, on opposite sides of the river.

This description would indicate that the site of the Harmony mission was about fifteen miles east of the Kansas-Missouri border; however, some historians assert that the mission was closer to the junction of the Marais des Cygnes and the Little Osage.

One legend about the name of the river was used by Longfellow in his poem *Evangeline*. The heroine of the poem left the Acadian settlements in Louisiana about 1768 and traveled northwest to find her sweetheart, Gabriel Lajeunesse, who was believed to be living with French trappers and traders. Evangeline's travels took her across the Ozark Mountains into the plains of Kansas, where she is supposed to have visited the Osage Indians. According to the legend, she gave the name Marais des Cygnes to the river when she visited an Indian village not far from the present site of Pleasanton.

Whittier also wrote of the river in his poem "Le Marais du Cygne," which relates the story of the massacre which took

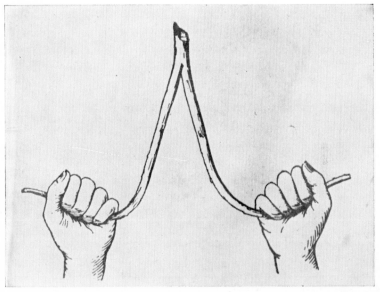

An ordinary divining rod held in the usual manner

place on the river on May 19, 1858. On that day a group of proslavery men, led by Charles A. Hamelton, captured eleven antislavery settlers from Linn County, forced them into the valley, and shot them. In Whittier's poem the name of the river is given in the singular. So far as is known, this is the only instance when the singular form of the name has been used.

One of the first Americans to use the name was the Reverend Isaac McCoy, who was named a special government commissioner in 1828 and asked to make an exploratory trip into the country west of Missouri. Reverend McCoy was accompanied by representatives of the Potawatomi and Ottawa tribes, who were to serve as guides. The missionary and his party moved up the south side of the Missouri River to a point near the mouth of the Grand River and followed that stream into Kansas and beyond its source to the Neosho. On September 4, 1828, McCoy wrote in his journal: "We did not stop until evening when we encamped on the Miry Desein—or Miry Swan River, which is the main branch of the Osage River, a sluggish, muddy stream, though we are encamped on a limestone bank and at a pretty ripple." On September 7 he wrote: "We remain in camp on the south bank of the Miry Desein or the Osage River."[2] Obviously, McCoy was spelling the word as the Indian guides pronounced it.

Kansas was not officially surveyed by the United States government until 1854. Until the region was organized as a territory and a form of government was set up, only such surveys were made as were necessary to establish the boundaries of the Indian reservations. On the early surveys the headwaters of the Marais des Cygnes were not given a name.

J. C. Mohler, secretary of the state board of agriculture for many years, and Cecil Howes entered into a conspiracy to get the name of the river restored many years ago, when they discovered that oil companies were furnishing road maps using the name Osage. Although the oil companies were willing to

[2] *Kansas Historical Quarterly*, Vol. V (1936), 246–48.

change the maps when they were shown the statute legalizing the French name, the map-makers discovered that the committee on geographic names had called the stream the Osage and felt they must use that name for the sake of uniformity.

Then it was suggested that the state seek an injunction against the use of the maps. The oilmen then promised to help Mohler and Howes get the name changed. A number of oilmen, together with former governors and members of Congress from Kansas, furnished suggestions and assistance, but it was Jake Mohler who spearheaded the campaign. "Cece" Howes gathered ammunition, in the form of historical records and legends, which Mohler fired at the committee in continuous salvos until he secured results. George Robb, state auditor and registrar of the land office, checked the original government surveys and discovered that the river runs through or touches twenty-three Kansas townships in five counties. In only five of these townships, most of which are in Miami County, was the river called the Osage. In fourteen townships it was called the Marais des Cygnes. In four townships the surveys showed both names. It was further disclosed that the original surveys used the name Marais des Cygnes in three townships in Bates County, Missouri.

A good deal of the opposition to the French name stemmed, of course, from its unfamiliar spelling and pronunciation. As proof of this point, the Kansas statute which prohibits the circulation of maps not using the name Marais des Cygnes spells the name of the river incorrectly. When the bill was under discussion in the legislature thirty years ago, many legislators could not or would not use the correct pronunciation. Moreover, for many years the state circulated a railroad map which further confused the issue by giving the name Marais des Cygnes to the river as far east as Ottawa and calling it the Osage River from Ottawa to the Missouri line.

The final chapter to the affair came in 1932, when a group of army engineers in charge of flood-control work along the streams included the following statement in their annual report: "The portion of the river in Kansas is officially designated as the Marais des Cygnes." The long dispute over the name had ended at last—though doubtless there will always be confusion attending its spelling and pronunciation.

33: *Some Laws to Laugh at*

A GOOD MANY PEOPLE seem to feel an inner compulsion to laugh whenever Kansas is brought into the conversation. Undoubtedly, this reaction stems from the colorful history of the state and its people, which is particularly evident in some of the deliberately or inadvertently freakish laws incorporated into the statute books.

Kansas has had several good laughs on itself through the state legislature. Occasionally, proposals made by the legislators were intended to bring into sharper focus a situation which could be most effectively improved by a humorous approach. For example, Rule 81 made by one legislature reads, "Don't take it too damned seriously."

A classic example of a statute made ridiculous by grammatical carelessness is the following section from the hotel-regulation law:

All carpets and equipment in offices and sleeping rooms of hotels in this state, including walls and ceiling, must be well plastered and be kept in a clean and sanitary condition at all times.

That particular mistake got by 125 representatives and 40 senators and remained in the statutes for many years.

The "Grasshopper Army" law, enacted in 1877 has also

been called freak legislation. Undoubtedly it was an unwork-able and impractical law and seems so especially today. Yet at the time it represented a serious attempt to combat a fearful scourge.

Some years ago the legislature passed a law requiring that all cans containing gasoline be painted red. A hundred-dollar fine was to be assessed anyone who failed to comply with the law. When the bill came up for consideration, a facetious member of the legislature offered the following substitute for the title of the bill: "An act for the protection of hired girls, especially those of the red-headed variety."

Everybody laughed and voted for the substitution, which a conscientious clerk then placed on the enrolled copy of the bill and signed by the governor. Later the bill was recalled, and the title was changed to its original wording.

In 1903, when automobiles were coming into use in Kansas, the state passed its first law regulating their movement on the highways. Section 1 of the law is quoted below:

That the term automobile and motor vehicle as used in this act shall be construed to include all types and grades of motor vehicles propelled by electricity, steam, gasoline or other source of energy, using the public highways and not running on rails or tracks. Nothing in this act shall be construed as in any way preventing, obstructing, impeding, embarrassing, or in any other manner or form infringing upon the prerogative of any political chauffeur to run an automobilious band wagon at any rate of speed he sees fit, compatible with the safety of the occupants thereof; provided, however, that not less than ten nor more than twenty ropes be allowed at all times to trail behind this vehicle when in motion, in order to permit those who have been fortunate enough to escape with their political lives an opportunity to be dragged to death; and provided further, that whenever a mangled and bleeding political corpse implores for mercy, the driver of the vehicle, shall, in accordance with the provisions of this bill, "throw out the life line."

That section became part of the law and remained on the Kansas statute books for ten years.

In the early years of the social-security system, one particular member of the house objected to the principle that the taxpayers provide pensions for the aged and that workers and employers pay taxes for unemployment and old-age security. Convinced that the taxpayer was being imposed on, the member introduced a bill which provided:

That every person who has paid taxes in the state of Kansas for a period of at least one year, and who has reached the ripe old age of fifty-five, upon filing application therefor with the state social welfare board, shall be paid a monthly pension of not less than seventy-five dollars a month. All such pensions shall be paid from the state school aid fund and no liens shall attach to the property of any person so receiving a pension, nor shall any recovery clause be applicable to any person so receiving such a pension.

The same legislature was also conscious of the calls being made on the public treasuries for relief of various kinds. Representative Donald Stewart of Independence introduced a bill aimed at the "campaign promisers," which read:

It shall be unlawful for any person, group of persons, or political organizations to manufacture, concoct or brew, transport, publish, use, hawk, vend, sell, or attempt to sell within the state of Kansas any political platform containing any pledge or promise, the performance or payment of which will be obtained, if obtained at all, at the expense of the general public: *Provided, however,* That nothing in this act shall be construed as prohibiting the practice of pointing with pride or viewing with alarm any or all past performances, it being the purpose of this act to provide for and encourage the seeking and the obtaining of public office by persons and political parties on the basis of such past performances rather than on future promises.

In the days when it was the custom to create boards of examiners for various professions, several legislative members came up with a bill to create a board of examiners for farmers. But the tillers of the soil were no longer to be called farmers. Henceforth they would be "agriculturists." A board was to be set up to conduct examinations and issue certificates stating that since "Farmer Bill Snort" had been actively farming the old home place for sixty years or more and had made a satisfactory grade in farm practices, he was declared to be an "agriculturist." The politicians who promised various farm programs at public expense were not expected to be very happy over special provisions inserted in the bill for their benefit:

Nothing contained in this act shall prevent any candidate for office from befriending the farmer as long or as loud as he can or from supervising the erection, enlargement or alteration of any farm program or project or any parts thereof to be constructed by the candidate at his own expense: *Provided*, That the working drawings for such project are signed by the authors thereof with a true statement thereon of their relation to such project and that the makers are not agriculturists and have no right to engage in saving or befriending the farmer at public expense, but no politician shall advocate the remodeling or repairing of any farm program or project previously designed, discovered, invented or first publicly advocated by another politician; nor shall said act apply to the planning, supervision, constructing, remodeling or repairing of any privately owned farm program, unless such farm program has been publicly advocated before an assembly of more than twenty people.

An ultrareligious member of the legislature once introduced a bill to put the Ten Commandments into the Kansas statutes. On another occasion a member who objected to the short skirts worn by women in the years before World War I introduced the so-called "patella" bill which prohibited any woman from appearing in public in a skirt which did not extend at least four inches below the kneecap, or patella. The same member introduced a bill which would prohibit any woman from appearing in public wearing tights. Neither bill left the committees, although the member introduced both in all seriousness.

An antismoking bill in cafés was introduced by a woman member of the legislature, but a male legislator discovered that if the bill were enacted in the form presented, it would prohibit even the stoves in the cafés from smoking, a prohibition which seemed somewhat unreasonable.

A state senator once introduced a bill which authorized police officers to imprison or fine any person who destroyed the confidence of little children by telling them that Santa Claus was a myth.

Another senator, irked by the fact that certain brands of expensive cigars were bedecked with bands which stuck to the wrapper, presented a bill prohibiting cigar bands.

Many of the laws laughingly dismissed as freaks at the time they were enacted have since become reputable laws, not only in Kansas but in many other states as well. Forty years ago, people throughout the country were amused by the Kansas anti-affinity law, which provided that if a man or woman departed from home and family to live with one to whom he or she had not been legally married, the offending spouse could be imprisoned. Today most states have child-abandonment laws which are very similar.

The first state legislation was enacted by the "bogus" legislature, which met at Pawnee in 1855 and later adjourned to the Shawnee Mission. The legislature received its nickname because many of the members were elected by large numbers of proslavery advocates who had moved into the new territory in order to control the elections. This legislature enacted some of the most severe laws ever passed by a state government.

Many of the laws were repealed when the free-state advocates gained control of the legislature. But in 1855 a man could be put to death for helping a slave to escape. He could be imprisoned at hard labor for joining the free-state party in Kansas, for reading the *New York Tribune*, for writing or printing statements in opposition to the slave laws, for speaking in public against slave ownerships, or for befriending or protecting any antislavery or free-state man.

In recent years, state officials have wisely created a "reviser of statutes" office, where Kansas laws are scrutinized and changes are suggested. The legislature, as a result, has removed many provisions and statutes which are no longer effective or applicable and has revised wording that once brought laughter.

34: *The Water-Witching Vogue*

WATER WITCHING is among the most ancient rites known to man. The practice of finding water by means of a stick and a divine sixth sense has been common even in recent years, in the face of the most concerted opposition of scientists in general and government and state geologists in particular.

As a matter of fact, geologists have long been engaged in mapping ground-water supplies and routing the subterranean streams. Many of these rivers are now so definitely marked that a layman can easily determine the most likely place to find water. Even so, the man with a dowsing stick is still frequently called on to try his hand at finding water for a farmer in need.

During the drought years the water witches enjoyed a lucrative business, when farmers and even municipal leaders called on them in desperation. The level of the water table went down an average of twenty-three feet during the dry years, and wells which had supplied abundant quantities of water for as long as the oldest "sovereign squat" could remember went "dry as a bone."

The state and national governments dug many community wells to supply water for livestock and farm homes. The state and federal officials administering the W.P.A. projects were skeptical of the water witches, although the latter were generally rather skillful at guessing where water was likely to occur.

The United States Geological Survey issued a pamphlet on water witching and included a bibliography of the most important works on the subject. The first book mentioned in the list was published before 1532. It was Philippe Melanchthon's *Discourse sur la Sympathie*, "Discourse on Sympathy" or "Sympathetic Affinity." But so far as can be learned from these publications, none of the dowsers or water witches ever equaled Moses' feat, when he smote the rock with his rod and water gushed forth for the children of Israel.

The use of divining rods, dowsing sticks, forked twigs, arrows, and metal rods to find water and minerals goes far back into history. The modern adaptation seems to have appeared first in Germany in the sixteenth century, when Melanchthon asserted that the twigs of trees standing above mineral veins drooped downward, attracted by the deposit below. He claimed that miners in the Harz Mountains put the idea into use, hopefully hunting for minerals with the forked, ore-seeking twigs. The idea soon spread to England, when German miners were imported to Cornwall by Queen Elizabeth. Water witching is also mentioned in the *Life of Saint Theresa of Spain*:

Theresa in 1568 offered the site for a convent to which there was only one objection—there was no water supply; happily a Friar Antonio came up with a twig in his hand, stopped at a certain spot, and appeared to be making the sign of the cross; but Theresa says:

"Really I cannot be sure if it was the sign he made, at any rate he made some movement with the twig and then he said:

" 'Dig just here.' "[1]

the account goes on to tell that the workmen dug where the friar directed, and a plentiful fount of water gushed forth."

It is often said that about one person in ten has the "power" of divining. It evidently makes very little difference what sort of divining stick is used; it may be cut from hazel, peach, willow, or any of a number of other woods. The diviner with the "power" can cut a forked stick from any tree that pleases his fancy and proceed to find water. Agricola stated that the twig would twist when one's feet were "on the vein."

J. G. Frazer wrote in *The Golden Bough* that the procuring of the hazel twig was a rite in itself:

If you would procure the mystic wand you must go to the hazel by night on midsummer eve, walking backward, and when you have come to the bush you must silently put your hands between your legs and cut a forked-shaped stick. That stick will be the divining rod and as such will detect buried treasure in the ground. If you have any doubt as to the quality of the wand you have only to hold it in water. If it squeaks like a pig—good.

Another record asserts that in Germany the divining rod was customarily cut from a hazel bush between eleven and twelve o'clock of St. John's night. While cutting the rod the dowser would say, "God greet thee, thou noble twig. With God, the Son, I find thee."

Doubtless most of the water witches are sincere in their belief in the effectiveness of the forked stick, and they have many supporters, the opinion of scientists notwithstanding. Many water witches once made a substantial stipend by going about the country water witching for a fee, but others who

[1] Arthur J. Ellis, "The Divining Rod: A History of Water Witching," *U. S. Geological Survey* (1917), 15.

had the "power" performed their services as a friendly and neighborly act in their communities. Italy and Germany once had divining-rod societies organized for the study and exchange of opinions and methods.

While the water witchers, both male and female, declared they had no preferences about the wood, they did insist that the stick must be full of live pith to be effective. Further, they insisted on cutting a fresh, sappy twig just before they started their operations.

J. T. Lovewell of Washburn College made a study of the pseudo-science and reported to the Kansas Academy of Science as follows:

From time immemorial, at least for hundreds of years, there has existed a widespread belief that certain persons have the ability to discover underground streams of water through the agency of a forked twig of witch-hazel, peach or willow, which, held in a certain way ,is moved downward on passing over a subterranean stream or body of water.

The forked twig is not essential, for a watch, suspended by its chain, or any heavy body similarly supported pendulum-wise, will, it is said, set up vibrations on being carried over subterranean water. We had in Topeka a believer in water witching, who found his carriage whip held by its slender end was an effective indicator of water, bowing down under its influence.

The common name with us for persons who thus locate wells is water-witches. In England they call them dowsers or dippers, while in France they are termed sourciers, or discoverers of sources. The Germans have a term with similar meaning, wasser finders. Their business is important enough so that we call it a trade. They commonly are persons with little pretention to culture or scientific knowledge and it is surprising how many who want a well dug are willing to contribute a fee for witching it.

In England the water witches were known as "dowsers," hunting for water or minerals was called "dowsing," and the stick was termed a "dowsing stick." Dowsers in this country objected to being called "witches" or "witchers" and much preferred the name "water locaters" or even "twig wielders."

A number of the witches who operated in the Middle West in an earlier day claimed to have been taught their trade by the Indians. Others asserted that the practice came from India, where for many years the city of Bombay had an official dowser, whose duty it was to find likely sites for the citizens.

Sharp rifts have been caused in church circles by the water witches and their twigs. Many clergymen believed that water witching was the work of the devil and forbade members of their churches to employ the witches. Other ministers did not think the use of a divining rod was wicked if it was successful and declined to join in a ban on the practice. In England, Moby and Franklin asserted that the practice was not a fake. "The working basis of divining is the nerves and muscles of the operator," they reported.

Bliss Isely, Kansas author and historian, wrote about the successful operations of a water witch in his book of memoirs, *Sunbonnet Days*.[2] The Isely family had just moved to a farm near Fairview. The Reverend S. D. Storrs, a Congregational minister, happened along as the Iselys were discussing where to dig their well. The minister told them he had inherited from his father the gift of finding water, or "smelling water," as he called it, and offered to help them. The minister cut a hazel twig and walked about until he found a likely spot. The well was dug and produced an abundant supply of water. Many similar accounts of successful water witching may be found in Kansas newspapers.

The bulletin of the United States Geological Survey also listed several other purposes to which the divining rod had been put, among them the finding of lost landmarks, the detecting of criminals, the analysis of character, the prevention and cure of diseases, and the tracing of lost animals. Patents on the instruments have been issued in many countries, including the United States.

[2] Caldwell, Idaho, The Caxton Printers, Ltd., 1935.

Yesterday and Today

In *Transactions of the American Institute of Mining Engineers*, published seventy years ago, scientist R. W. Raymond wrote:

To this, then, the rod of Moses, of Jacob, of Mercury, or Circe, of Valentin, of Beausoliel, of Vallemont, of Aymar, of Bleton, of Pennet, of Campetti, even of Mr. Latimer [another scientist] has come at last. In itself it is nothing. It claims its virtues derived from the Deity, from Satan, from affinities and sympathies, from corpuscular effluvia, from electrical currents, from passive perturbatory qualities of organo-electric force are hopelessly collapsed and discarded. A whole library of learned rubbish about it which remains to us furnishes jargon for charlatans, marvelous tales for fools, and amusement for antiquarians. And the sphere of the divining rod has sunk with its authority. In one department after another it has been found useless. Even in the one application left to it with any show of reason it is nothing unless held in skilful hands, and whoever has the skill may dispense with the rod. It belongs with the magic pendulum and planchette among the toys of children.

From Mr. Raymond's remarks it may be assumed that engineers and scientists even then were much opposed to water witching. But the fact remains that there are many active and successful water witches in the country today, all of whom have their following.

35: *Successful Experiments that Failed*

THAT PARADOXICAL description can be applied to several projects which flourished for a time in Kansas. One successful failure was the short-lived sorghum-sugar industry, which has been discussed earlier. Another important experiment was the cultivation of the castor bean and the production of castor oil. The crop was easy to grow, and in 1879 Kansas produced 35,242,578 pounds of castor beans, more than one-third of the total United States production. The supply of beans was consequently too large for the market, and the crop was gradually abandoned.

Kansas has also grown buckwheat, hemp, flax, and other marginal crops that seemed fitted to the climate and the soil, but the market was inadequate for these crops also, and many of them were abandoned after a few years.

By far the most successful failure of all these experiments was the silk industry. For a few years Kansas produced a high-quality silk, while the state paid a bounty and conducted extensive experiments in silk-production. But silk culture didn't pay, and the business finally disappeared.

Keeping the silkworms contented was the major problem. The Chinese and the Japanese could carry out the entire program so much more cheaply that Kansas-grown silk could not be sold at premium prices. Moreover, a typical Kansas blizzard could be deadly for the most carefully nurtured silkworms.

Ernest Valeton de Boissiere is believed to have been the first commercial producer of silk in Kansas. De Boissiere, who had produced silk in France, came to Kansas in 1868 and bought three thousand acres of land in Franklin County, where he established a socialist colony made up of silkworm experts and farm operators from France. At the colony the silk was spun on reels ready for the thread and cloth manufacturers. The operation was quite successful for some years, until the workers discovered that they could make more money operating their own farms. Then they gradually departed from the Silkville Colony and began farming on their own account.

When his scheme failed, De Boissiere gave the land and buildings to a board of trustees to be made into a home for orphans of Odd Fellows. After the Odd Fellows had contributed a large sum to the home it was discovered that the fraternal order had no title to the property and could exercise only minor control. Then De Boissiere's sister, who had remained in France, brought suit to obtain the property, and Topeka lawyers obtained the title from her and won the litigation.

The Mennonites, who came to Kansas from southern Russia in 1874, brought along silkworms, as well as the hard red turkey wheat that was destined to make Kansas the greatest wheat-producing state in the country. The worms lived on the leaf of the Osage orange trees, the great bushes that were used so extensively as fences throughout Kansas. The Mennonites produced silk of fair quality after they settled in Kansas but gave up the project after a few years.

At the Philadelphia Exposition in 1876 the Silkville Colony set up an elaborate display of silks produced in Kansas and won several blue ribbons. The exhibit may still be seen in the museum of the Kansas Historical Society. Included in the exhibit was a large sunflower made of Kansas-grown silks and a banner proclaiming that Kansas could produce silks to equal the finest produced anywhere in the world.

The reports of the state board of agriculture indicate that at various times until about 1890 silk was produced in forty-six counties in the state. The quality was sufficiently high that the Belding Brothers Company, one of the major American manufacturers of silk, offered a bounty of 20 per cent over the market price for the Kansas product. The state itself paid a bounty for silk and also for silkworms grown in the state.

The Mennonite and Silkville projects had been so successful that the 1885 legislature named a special commission to study the industry and submit its recommendations on state aid for the project. The committee was headed by J. H. Morse of Peabody, and J. S. Codding of Louisville and Dr. Charles Williamson of Washington, D. C., were the other members. The committee visited various silk-producing farms in Kansas and other states and made an elaborate report to the legislature to the effect that sericulture could be made into one of the largest farm enterprises in the state.

The report also pointed out that it was difficult for farmers to obtain adequate supplies of silkworms and mulberry seed and suggested that the legislature provide funds for an experimental farm, where mulberry seedlings and silkworms would be grown for distribution to the farmers. The committee members believed that in a few years the experimental farm would be entirely self-supporting.

The state-operated silk farm was established at Peabody in 1887. An appropriation of thirteen thousand dollars was provided to pay the expenses for two years, and additional funds were provided two years later. The farm was to have been established at Larned, but negotiations for land there failed, and Peabody offered the state ten acres for the silk farm. The land was planted to mulberry trees, and a building for the worm culture was erected. The farm was situated about forty rods north of U. S. Highway 50-S, where it crosses the northern edge of Peabody. The original building was later moved to the adjoining farm on the west when the project was abandoned and is now used as a barn.

I. Horner was the first superintendent of the farm. Instead of devoting his efforts to cultivating seeds and silkworms, he manufactured silk and sent enough cloth to a weaver to be made into a dress for the wife of Governor John A. Martin. When the commission learned of the gesture Horner was fired, and

One of the outlets at Waconda (Great Spirit) Springs
near Cawker City, Kansas

Courtesy Kansas Industrial Development Commission

the statement was made that the experimental farm was to produce mulberry trees and cocoons only and was not to conduct an independent silk-producing project.

Although the next legislature did provide funds for continuing the project another two years, succeeding legislatures failed to take any interest in silk production, and after about 1890 the industry waned.

36: *Feasts of Plenty*

MANY AN old-timer in Kansas has expressed disgust at the sparse menus of modern households and restaurants. For the old-timers loved to eat in quantity, and tales of meals served eighty years ago in the Sunflower State are often written off as elaborate falsehoods.

When the Nineteenth Kansas Regiment was organized and Governor S. J. Crawford resigned his office to become colonel of the regiment and engage in a winter campaign against marauding Indians, a Thanksgiving feast was held at Camp Supply in the Indian Territory (now in Oklahoma). Here is the menu presented by the company cooks on that day:

Wild Turkey Soup.
Boiled: Wild turkey, buffalo tongue.
Roasts: Buffalo hump, wild turkey, saddle of venison, red deer, antelope, rabbit
Entrees: Rabbit pies, wings of grouse breaded, turkey giblets.
Broiled: Quail, pinnated grouse.
Vegetables: Canned tomatoes, lima beans, desiccated potatoes.
Bread: Hard tack, plain and toasted, army biscuits.
Desserts: Rice pudding, pies, tarts.
Wines and liquors: Whisky, ale, champagne.

The volunteers had killed the game items on the menu, and the Regular Army officers furnished the canned fruits and vegetables and the wines and liquors.

During the pioneer days in Kansas, beef was almost unknown to the settlers. Bacon, salt pork, buffalo, and antelope were fairly plentiful, and occasionally a good hunter might bring home an elk.

Another important food item was the sand plum. Often those hard, wormy, bitter plums were the only fruit available. At feasts held by the Indians for army officers, government commissioners, or settlers, the first course was stewed sand plums. The fruit also served as appetizer, relish, and dessert.

The first of the tremendous feasts held by Kansas pioneers was the one at Fort Scott in 1867 on the tenth anniversary of the founding of the town. Fort Scott had been established as a military post to protect the movement of troops and supplies from Fort Leavenworth to Fort Gibson and also to protect the settlers in western Missouri from Indian attacks. A village of size and importance grew up around the fort, and in 1857 the town became an entity.

Everyone was invited to the celebration, and the dancing and feasting began early and continued until late. C. W. Goodlander, one of the earliest residents of Fort Scott and an active business and civic leader, listed the menu of that midnight supper in his memoirs, passing over such inconsequentials as French accents and conformist spellings.[1]

[1] Charles Wesley Goodlander, "Memoirs and Recollections of Early Days in Ft. Scott," *Ft. Scott Monitor* (1900).

PIONEER SUPPER
Wilder House
FORT SCOTT, KANSAS
November 14, 1867

Twelve O'clock Supper

Soup
Oyster   Colbert

Fish
Baked Black Bass   Broiled Red-Horse

Relieve
Broiled Leg of Mutton, Caper Sauce
Wild Turkey, Braised with Oysters
Ham, Champagne Sauce
Broiled Prairie Chicken, Parsley Sauce
Rib of Antelope, a la Regeance
Buffalo Tongue

Cold Ornamental Dishes
Chaudfroid of Faisant, a la Parisienne
Patties de foie Gras, with Jelly
Bastion of Rabbits, a la Shiloh
Beef Tongue, a la Carlotta
Boned Turkey, decorated with Jelly
Boned Partridge, a la Pawnee
Brandt, ornamented with Jelly
Sunfish au Beurre, de Montpelier

Entrees

Rissoles of Jack Snipe, a la Pompadour
Fillet of Curlew, a la Rouenaise
Civit of Venison, with Port Wine
Fillet of Wild Goose, a la Marmaton
Fillet of Teal Duck, a la Drywood
Fillet of Plover, a la Prairie
White Crane Salad, a l'Osage
Woodcock Fricassee, a la Wolverine
Noix of Fawn, a la Balltown
Coon Chops, a la Marais des Cygnes
Sweetbread, a la Toulouse

Roasts

Opossum with per-simmon jelly	Canvas-back Duck	Wild Turkey
	Saddle Venison	Gray Duck
Butter-ball Duck	Red-head Duck	Buffalo
Black Bear	Gray Squirrel	Mallard
Gray Duck	Fox Squirrel	Brandt
Sage Hen	Wood Duck	Goose
Crane	Killdeer	Beef

Pastry

Persimmon Pyramid	Cocoanut Pyramid
American Dessert	Canteloupe rum sauce
Mince Pie	Strawberry Ice Cream
Dewberry Jelly	Champagne Jelly
Pumpkin Pie	Pretzels
Paw-Paw pies	Horn of Plenty

Dessert

Wild Fox Grapes	Butter Nuts	Pecans
Black Walnuts	Bush Cherries	Apples
Hazel Nuts	Paw Paws	Coffee

WINE LIST

Champagne
Robinson & Company's Dry Verzenay
J. Sattler & Company's Green Sea Imperial
J. S. Redfield & Company's Dry Sillery
J. S. Redfield & Company's Imperial
Linn & Stadden's Sillery Mouseaux
A. McDonald & Bros. Monopole
Van Fossen Bros. Gold Seal
Dr. J. H. Couch's Verzenay
Dr. B. F. Hepler's Cabinet
C. Haynes' Royale Rose

Claret
Table, Medoc, Floirac (D. Marie & Freres and
Brandenburg, Freres), St. Julien, Chateau,
Chateau Yquem, Chateau Lafitte, Chateau Griscoms

California Wine
Angelica, Los Angelos Vintage
California Port, Muscatel and Hock

Kansas Wine
Southern Kansas Wine Company
Imperial, W. T. Campbell's Vintage
Sparkling Catawba, Spring River Vineyard
H. B. Hart's Seedling "Bergunday"
Still Catawba (very still, no noise)

Ale and Porter
Hack's Imported (Leavenworth) Ale
Newberry's London Porter

The hardy pioneers believed in eating well and took pains to give the food "window dressing" through the use of fancy names and styles of cooking. The record does not show that there were any French chefs in the state at the time who could prepare the sauces and foods listed on the menu. But their absence probably made little difference to the celebrants, whose chief care was that they did not gorge themselves trying to sample everything.

The next party noted for the quality and quantity of food provided was the state luncheon given in honor of the Grand Duke Alexis of Russia on January 22, 1872, in Topeka. This feast was the last of the tremendous displays of provender, and, incidentally, it was the last state dinner given in Kansas.

The Grand Duke Alexis was a noted hunter in his native land and had made hunting trips into Asia and Africa in search of big game. He came west to hunt American bison under the auspices of the United States government and traveled in a special train, accompanied by army and government officials and a large entourage of his own. The party hunted buffalo in Nebraska and Colorado and then moved into western Kansas. Between Fort Wallace, Kansas, and Kit Carson, Colorado, the party found a great herd of buffalo, and the hunt did not stop until two hundred buffalo had been killed by Alexis and his friends. The hunters then proceeded eastward over the Kansas Pacific Railroad to Topeka, where they were received and royally feasted by Governor Harvey and the members of the legislature. The menu for the luncheon follows:

Soup
Oyster, a la Posset, chicken, with rice

Fish
Boiled White Fish, a la Maitre d'hotel

Boiled
Pressed Corn Beef, Leg of Mutton, Caper Sauce
Chicken, Egg Sauce, Ham, Pickled Pork, Tongue

Cold
Corn Beef, Pork, Chicken Salad, Ham,
Lobster Salad, Calf's Tongue

Relishes
Chow-chow, Piccalilli, Mixed Pickles, Cauliflower, Gherkins,
Club Sauce, Worcestershire Sauce, Pickled Oysters,
Celery, Cheese

Game
Buffalo, Rabbit, Venison, Moose, Squirrel, Elk, Bear,
Quail, Duck, Turkey, Prairie Chicken, Antelope

Entrees
Chicken Wings, Fricassed
Queen Fritters, a la Princess
Pigs Feet, Breaded
Scalloped Oysters, a la Stanton
Quail on Toast
Rabbits a la Chesseau
Tenderloin of Beef, a la Royal
Oyster Patties, a la Rhine
Macaroni, aux Gratin
Rice Croquettes, with jelly
Prince Albert Pancakes, with Quince
Jelly, Liver, a la Bonaparte
Harriot of Mutton, a la Bourgeois
Squirrel crumbed and fried
Deviled Ham, a la Stabenne

Roasts
Turkey, Cranberry Sauce, Leg of Mutton, Mallard Duck,
  a la Mateloite
Ribs of Beef, Chicken, Oyster Dressing, Buffalo, Brown
  Sauce, Ham
Champagne Sauce, Antelope, Grape Jelly, Elk, Currant Jelly

Vegetables
Boiled Potatoes, green peas, string beans, parsnips, lima beans,
  tomatoes, cabbage, mashed potatoes, brown potatoes, hominy,
  mashed turnips, succotash, corn

Pastry and Pudding
Plum pie, strawberry pie, mince pie, peach pie, pound cake,
  pudding, cranberry tarts, fruit cake, ornamented cranberry
  pie, gold cake, jelly roll, pound cake, iced and ornamented,
  drop kisses, cocoanut tops, rose jelly cake, lady fingers,
  silver cake, marble cake, Leopard cake

Dessert
Vanilla ice cream, almonds, oranges, pecans, apples, wine jelly,
  crab apple jelly, brandy jelly, quince jelly, French coffee, tea

The luncheon was served at the Fifth Avenue Hotel, the largest and swankiest hotel in the state. The affair produced a classic, though perhaps apocryphal, anecdote. The state seal of Kansas played a prominent part in the decorations for the luncheon, and during the meal the Grand Duke was observed to be studying the seal and audibly spelling out the state motto, "Ad Astra Per Aspera." Lieutenant-Governor P. P. Elder, a host to the royal party, sought to be helpful and said in the purest Kansas language and with complete informality, "Duke, them words is Latin." "Thank you," the Grand Duke replied, "I thought so."

37: *Tall Tales from the Short Grass*

Kansans have always enjoyed hyperbole, even when it reflects somewhat upon themselves. In fact, many Kansans are not in the least averse to telling an outright lie, when it will get a laugh or outdo the previous yarn. Western Kansas is particularly rich in such tales, and newspapers in the region still publish them for the edification of the local citizenry.

The Arkansas and the Cimarron rivers are dry most of the year. But occasionally they go on rampages of short duration that cause great damage to the countryside. One of the favorite yarns that breaks out with some regularity is the one about the motorist and his party who drove up to the ferry-crossing of the Arkansas River. The ferryboat was resting on a sand bar, and there wasn't enough water in the river to float a skiff, let alone a ferry with a motorcar.

After a time the ferryman drove up in a wagon with a water tank. He backed the team around, opened the spigot on the tank, and emptied the water into the river by his ferry. The motorists waited four hours while he hauled water to the river until there was enough to float his ferry and enable him to transport the car and its passengers across the stream.

The *Grant County Register* published a story about the Indian who wanted a picture made of his wife. While the photographer was posing the woman, the Indian ducked under the black cloth and gazed at his wife's reflection in the ground glass. She was standing on her head. The Indian snorted, emerged from under the cloth, and found his wife sitting calmly in the chair. He took another quick look in the ground glass, and there she was standing on her head again. That made the Indian so angry he grabbed his wife by the hair and dragged her out of the gallery. Once outside, he informed the photographer he didn't want a picture of any member of his family who persisted in playing tricks on him.

During the days when there was a toll bridge across the Arkansas River at Wichita, the city council asked the bridge tender why the bridge revenue had taken such a severe drop. "The water is so low that everybody is fording the river," the tollkeeper replied.

One day the *Dodge City Times* reported that a high wind had blown seven dollars out of the stocking of Alice Chambers, a friend of the cowboys. A diligent search produced only one dollar bill. "We had supposed that the Kansas wind was of a higher order and did not stoop to such larceny," said the *Times*. "The thing is settled now that under some circumstances even the wind can be found feeling around in forbidden paths."

The *Lakin Eagle* said:

Some states have high winds, but not Kansas. We have zephyrs. But a two-gallon funnel flaring end windward and gimlet end downward will collect enough of a Kansas zephyr in seven hours to drill a hole in solid rock 108 feet deep. We never dig wells in Kansas. Condensed wind does it for us.

Sometimes the farmers in the western part of the state complained that when the fish flopped from the streams into the wheat fields to eat some grass, the wind blew off the scales and left the meat dry, hard, and sunburned.

Crap shooters have many superstitions and devices to bring them good luck. The Kansas dicer puts a penny in his ear so he can hear the eagle scream. This practice is said to improve his chances of winning.

During the drought in 1936 firemen advised all housewives with fishbowls to move the bowls out of south or west windows. Bubbles in the glass were likely to become magnifying glasses, boil the water and the fish, and even set the house on fire.

It often happens during long hot spells that railroad tracks become so warped by the heat that trains are derailed. At Junction City an old hen was killed for a stew, but the sun hatched her eggs. At Erie an ice-cream container exploded, and the lid hit a passer-by over the eye and knocked him unconscious. Eleven stitches were taken in his head. Near White City several quarrymen miraculously escaped injury when a can of black powder exploded from the heat of the sun's rays. A man named Edwards was driving home from Emmett one hot summer day, when the top of his buggy suddenly burst into flames. Sun rays striking a bolt had caused the fire. Colonel J. W. F. Hughes, an early resident of Topeka and the hero of the Legislative War of 1893, made a practice for many years of frying eggs on the Topeka street-car rails in front of his office.

The *Kiowa Herald* printed this tale on January 8, 1885:
We find the following going the rounds of the eastern press:
"A Kansas man climbed to the top of a corn stalk before retiring, to inspect the state of the weather. His foot slipped, and he fell into a neighboring tree top, where he was suspended all night trying to die, and couldn't breathe only thirty cents on the dollar. After being rescued he kicked himself all the next day and promised his wife and seventeen kids that henceforth he would buy an almanac and keep himself posted without resorting to such dangerous methods of ascertaining the weather probabilities."
Coming from an eastern paper, we don't believe it. If he had fallen out of the top of a corn stalk in a field of Barber County corn, the blades would have been so thick and strong they would have sustained his weight, and he could reach the ground as easy as walking down a stepladder.

There have been years when the rural telephone companies have had to repair telephone wires short-circuited by tassels from tall-growing corn.

The blind catfish in the Arkansas River were made that way by dust kicked up by the fish in shallow water.

Near Dodge City one stormy day, a farmer was helping

his wife wash the dishes when there was a knock on the door. The man outside asked to be allowed to use the farmer's tool-shed while he put chains on his car. The farmer helped the man put on his chains, while the rain and hail pounded down. Soon the motorist drove off, and the farmer went back to his dish-washing. Before he had finished two girls came to the door asking for sanctuary. The dust was so thick they couldn't see to drive.

Moonshine mash and the fermented liquid in silos often caused rabbits and mice to do queer things. A few swigs of silo juice would make a jack rabbit so brave he would spit at a bulldog and kick the eyes out of a greyhound. And corn-liquor mash would make mice so reckless they would waltz out of their holes and challenge the cat to a fight.

There are many stories about farmers who got lost in their own wheat fields during a good growing year. In some years the wheat grew so tall that birds built their nests on the heads of the wheat. Farmers generally waited to cut down the wheat until the fledglings were old enough to take care of themselves.

F. J. Cloud, a Kingman editor, had the most intelligent toad ever created. The toad knew every member of the family and would follow them around like a pet, making a mewing or chirruping sound somewhat similar to that of a turtle. Every evening the toad would hop on the porch and nose around until someone turned on the porch light. When the toad had his fill of insects he pestered some member of the family until the light was turned off. When he was particularly pleased about something, the toad would do acrobatic stunts, standing on his forelegs and dangling his rear legs in the air. He could also turn handsprings. Then he would make a noise like a wampus cat. No one was able to discover where he hibernated, but he turned up regularly every spring.

Early motorists in Kansas had a good deal of trouble with the tire turtles, according to Leslie Wallace of the *Larned Tiller and Toiler*, until tire manufacturers learned to put carbon black into the tires and harden the rubber. The turtles still work on rubber heels; mechanics have lost the heels off both shoes to a tire turtle while they were changing a tire.

Charles Blakesley, editor of "Kansas Notes" in the *Kansas City Star*, had much to say about the cinder beetle that ruined many a railroad track by eating the cinder ballast and damaging rails and ties.

During the blizzard of 1886 and subsequent storms, when the snowdrifts were mountainous and communities were entirely cut off from the outside world, it was customary to restore contact on groundhog day. Everyone would be out early on that day to catch the groundhogs as they came out to gaze at the sun and look for their shadows. The groundhogs were put to work digging tunnels through the snowdrifts. Then the people would crawl through the tunnels to town or to a neighbor's house.

Grant Constable of Bennington was a professional fisherman in the Solomon River. His system was to find a catfish napping in the shade along the riverbank and tickle the fish until he had it hypnotized. "If your ears are good you can hear him purr, Just keep on tickling him until you can slip your hands into his gills, and the fish is yours."

Down along the Neosho, a fisherman once caught two large catfish in a net. He treated them well, and they seemed so friendly and eager to help him that he rigged a harness for them on the bottom of his boat and let them propel the boat for him as he attended to his trotlines and fish nets along the river. The fisherman fed them well, and they always greeted him with aquatic somersaults when he made his daily visit to the riverbank to run his fishing lines.

Tom Botkin, secretary of state for several years, told the story about the catfish in the Arkansas River that grew a sack under its chin which it filled with fresh water to drink when the river went dry.

Had enough? Now you tell one.

38: *Traveling under Wind Power*

NEVER LET it be said that Kansas has not done its share toward improving modes of transportation. Wind-driven vehicles were in use in Kansas in an early day, designed both for "sailing the prairies blue" and for rolling along the railroad tracks. Of course, the prairie sailors were wrecked a time or two, and often they had to resort to walking to their destination, when the Kansas zephyr became too boisterous or the operators of the prairie sail wagon failed to take some mechanical principle into consideration. Man's own ingenuity could doubtless overcome the latter, but the source of power, the prairie zephyr, is never completely reliable. It may be mild and friendly, or again it may turn wild and vicious. However, it is quite possible that with today's efficient weather reporting a wind-driven vehicle could be quite a success.

The *Oskaloosa Independent* had this to say about the prairie sail wagon on May 17, 1860:

Samuel Peppard constructed a sailing wagon, planned to travel in it to Pike's Peak. It was an ordinary light wagon, of 350 pounds, bed 3 by 8 feet by 6 inches deep. Over the center of the front axle was raised a mast with sail 9x11 feet. The steering apparatus resembled a boat tiller reversed.

On May 9 the wagon set out on a trial trip but was wrecked by a high wind. It was soon repaired and a party composed of Samuel Peppard, Steve Randall, J. T. Forbes and Gid Coldon set sail for the great prairies and Pike's Peak. They had about four hundred pounds of provisions and ammunition.

A Topeka paper also discussed Mr. Peppard's invention:

When he first began to build the wagon the wise men of Oskaloosa all laughed at him for wasting his time on such a craft, just as other wise men of Noah's time scoffed at the good patriarch. Mr. Peppard's advisors declared that if he attempted to navigate the craft he would certainly be killed, and the people generally looked the wagon over, shook their heads and called it "Peppard's folly." But Mr. Peppard kept on sawing wood and turning it into wheels and running gear and boards.

It was made of rough lumber and shaped like a skiff. It was eight feet long from prow to stern and and three feet across amidships, and two feet deep. The bed was placed on a running gear with axles six feet apart, the wheels all the same size and about as large as the front wheels of a buggy. A ten foot mast was fastened to the front axle, and came up through the bottom of the wagon box, and to this two sails were rigged; the larger eleven feet by eight, the other seven by five. They were both to be worked by a rope through a pulley at the top of the mast. If the wind was high the smaller was to be used and if it was low, the larger was to be employed. The wagon had a brake and a rudder for steering. The hounds, instead of having a tongue attached, came up over the top of the bed and were welded together. A bar was fastened here and extended backward three feet. There was a seat placed at the end of the bar for the captain and he steered by pushing the bar to the right or to the left. The craft rigged out weighed 350 pounds, carried a crew of four men, a cargo of 500 pounds, a camping outfit and provisions serving as ballast.

The site of the trial spin of the wind wagon was a mile south of Oskaloosa. "There is a level stretch of several miles and a good stiff breeze was on," relates one account. "When it struck the large sail the craft stuck its nose down near the ground and came near capsizing. He [Peppard] slacked sail and set out again with the large sheet reefed and the smaller full against the wind, and away it whizzed; it went so fast, in fact, that the boxing in the wheels heated. Then when it went over a little knoll, it leaped about thirty feet into the air and came down with a crash."

Undaunted, Peppard repaired the craft and set out for the Colorado gold fields. Here is his story, as recorded in the archives of the Kansas Historical Society:

Our best time was two miles in four minutes. We could not run faster than that rate as the boxing would have heated. One day we went fifty miles in three hours, and in doing so, passed 625 teams. There were, you know, a great many people en route for the gold fields in those days. This was an unusually good race. If we went ninety miles a day it was considered a good day's travel. Many amusing incidents happened and we had no little fun joking the teamsters as we flew by them.

On the fifth day out we had some sport with a band of Indians. It was about noon and we were traveling along probably at about ten or twelve miles an hour. The wind was blowing about 25 miles an hour but having been well shaken up by a rough stretch of the prairie, I had put on the brake and reefed my sail, so that we were journeying leisurely. A cloud of dust attracted our attention in the southeast and we decided to stop and wait. We thought it was a band of Indians who were drunk and would do us harm if we allowed them to overtake us. The Indians were not hostile, but when they were under the influence of "firewater," they were usually ugly. When we had finished our meal and smoked a pipeful apiece, the band of Indians had approached to within a mile of where we had stopped.

Strange to say they had not yet seen us. I cannot account for this unless it was because we were in a depression of the prairie and were not noticed. We were thoroughly covered with dust and this served to make us the same color as the road. Not caring to have them approach too near, I let the brake partially off and again resumed our journey. When we came out of the low place, and I spread the sail, we could plainly see each Indian rise in his saddle with a start of surprise. As quick as a flash, each mustang was put into a gallop and the band of what we thought were drunken Indians was bearing down upon us. I knew that we could outrun them with ease and so I gave myself no alarm. The wagon was just getting under way when snap went a bolt that held the brake. The brake was useless and the wind had risen until it was blowing thirty miles an hour. To give ourselves up to the wind with no means of checking our speed would be madness. To allow the Indians to catch us would result in the loss of our provisions and if they drank the brandy we had, might result in our being personally molested. Time was precious. I again reefed the sail and bidding my companions to follow my example, I jumped to the ground and seized a wheel. The wagon stopped. I seized a halter or rope that we had picked up on the road, to bind the broken brake. It would serve the purpose. If the delay was not too long we could yet escape. As quick as my hands would let me I made secure the brake and we were ready to start. The Indians were upon us, but fortunately, through suspicion or superstition, they had slackened their speed and were within one hundred yards of us, advancing cautiously. This allowed me to give sail to the wind slowly and thus not wreck the wagon. A fresh look of surprise upon the faces of the red men greeted our eyes as the wagon began to move and gradually increased its speed. If they had been curious at the appearance of the vehicle, they were now astonished at seeing it move. Just as they put their horses into a canter I released the brake and gave the full sail to the wind. Quick as a flash the little craft shot into the road and we were off at a pace of about thirty miles an hour. A wild whoop came from the throat of each Indian and as I saw them lean over their mustangs and lash the beasts into a dead run I realized the race was on.

They were not drunk, so the race, instead of being for plunder, resolved itself into one of rivalry. The wagon fairly leaped from the ground, under the strong wind, and the sail creaked and bent under the pressure upon it. I have seen excited jockeys, at the race track, urge their steeds on to victory, but never before did I see such earnestness and such horsemanship displayed, as did those red men as they leaned over their ponies and came tearing after us. The swiftest of them all was a brave who rode a little gray mare. She clearly outclassed the others and as she gradually drew away from them the race resolved itself into one with her alone. The other braves drew rein and rent the air with an unearthly yell to cheer their companion on. For about a mile we had a race that was exciting. The Indian leaned far over the mare and patted her neck. Again and again he called her name and urged her to catch the "white man."

The mare was fleet but the race was ours. The wind had risen higher and I was obliged to reef the sail to keep from being carried into the air. We were tearing over the cleanly swept road at a fearful pace. At last I saw that the mare was weakening and in order not to distance the brave I applied the brake to slacken our speed. The Indian seeing this, suddenly drew in the mare and exclaimed:

"Ugh! Red man ride horse. White man fly like bird."

About fifty miles northeast of Denver we were moving leisurely along when we saw a whirlwind approaching. We had encountered a number of these before and had only to let down the sail until they had passed and then to raise it again. On this occasion, the whirlwind was upon us before we were aware. It required quick action and I made a mistake in my hurry, that put the sail wagon past recall. The ropes that held the sail caught in the pulley. I gave it a jerk and it broke, leaving no means of lowering the sail. In an instant the whirlwind struck the wagon and carried it about twenty feet into the air. When the wagon came down it struck on the hind wheels and they broke down under the weight. By what seemed a miracle, none of us was hurt.

By the time we had gathered ourselves together we were surrounded by travelers who extended us invitations for a free ride for the remainder of the journey. A baggage train was not far behind and we cast our lot with it.

Kansas winds have also been used to drive handcars equipped with sails on the Kansas Pacific Railroad (now the Union Pacific). On November 29, 1877, the *Clay Center Dispatch* printed this paragraph:

A wind-power handcar, says the *Junction City Union*, sixteen feet in length, is now sailing on the Kansas Pacific. The sail is fifteen feet high, twelve feet wide at the bottom, ten at the top. It is controlled precisely as the sail of a sail boat, and by its means the car is always easily propelled except when the wind is dead ahead. With a good wind a speed of twenty-five miles an hour can be easily attained.

Victor Murdock used to tell about a man near Wichita who took the wheel off a windmill and fastened it to the rear axle of a spring wagon with gears and chains and connected a homemade steering apparatus to the front wheels. But the contraption was a failure because the windmill took so much wind to turn, and so much power was consumed by the gears and chains, that unless the wind was blowing fifteen to twenty miles an hour there was no power left to drive the wagon.

39: *Putting the Pieces Together*

HERE, then, are some of the segments of the Kansas story. They don't tell the whole of it—even the most systematic of books rarely does. But from these particulars, these impressions, the peculiar essence of an entirely unique state can be realized.

For, although Kansas is the product of fused influences and ideas, as indeed is the country of which she is the heart, the synthesis here has produced something new, something different. The phrase, "state of mind," no longer conveys the meaning that was once intended, neither for Kansas nor for any other state. But if Kansas possesses a distinctive character, and I feel very definitely that it does, it has got it by spiritual means more than any other. Her people are the special source of her distinctiveness.

The predominant number of her early settlers came to the state from neighboring areas of established, though new, culture. Later immigrants made their contribution to the temper and modes of existence in the new state; but the first pioneers were already imbued with the principles of democratic life; later settlers enhanced rather than altered those principles.

The early settlers contributed the special brand of courage and hardihood that developed in the Middle West, but, as has been noted by others, this quality was made greater in early-day Kansas affairs by a predominantly Puritan outlook—fortified and enhanced by conditions of settlement and the controversies which raged in the fifties over the slavery issue. Then, as now, a Kansan without opinion on the basic articles of faith, political, social, and economic, could hardly be called a Kansan.

The people of the early period solidified the pioneering spirit, the love of individualism coupled with a belief in unity under a law they themselves could provide, a healthy respect for a Nature they could thwart, if not defeat, a stubborness in facing odds they could count upon to be fierce, and the ingenuity to provide for themselves from what they had.

With all these qualities Kansas, past and present, has endowed her people. And her people have repaid from their bounty. When a hungry world clamored for food, Kansans provided sustenance; when subjugated races and peoples begged for sanctuary, Kansans made room for them; and when Nature did her best to drive them from their land, the people laughed and created myths.

You can't defeat a people like this. You can starve them, freeze them, and roast them, but in the end you have to admire them. From a wide expanse of "useless" prairie they cut a pattern of farms and cities and built a culture that contributes to the infinite variety from which, paradoxically, a more homogeneous America is developing in the twentieth century.

Index